THE
blender girl
SMOOTHIES

THE
blender girl
SMOOTHIES

100 gluten-free, vegan & paleo-friendly recipes

tess masters

photography by erin kunkel

TEN SPEED PRESS
Berkeley

contents

smoothie secrets

In a smoothie, I want fabulous flavor and nutritional power. Basic smoothies containing liquid, fruits, vegetables, and ice can be yummy, but super-simple blends often taste a bit flat and uninteresting. For me, a smoothie can be a meal, and I go to herbs, spices, greens, oils, and superfoods to create a dimensional drink that takes me on a flavor journey like a textured dish. For information about these smoothie-enhancers, see The Smoothie Pantry (page 219).

Other than grazing in your produce drawer, nothing's healthier and faster than making a smoothie—perfect for kids, beginner cooks, and busy people on the run.

Eating fruits and vegetables this way is more fun, too. Blending them into smoothies gives you endless flavor combinations, and the best part is that it's almost impossible to mess things up! Whether you're making a nutritious meal replacement, a protein-powered workout booster, or a dessert shake, you can be bold and creative. Throw ingredients into your blender knowing that, in most cases, you can rescue a gag-worthy experimental brew with fruit, sweetener, or a bit of chocolate—and tweak flavors right up to the moment of serving.

But, some exotic concoctions blend up into what looks like a big glass of death, with an unpalatable sickly tinge and a mealy or sludgy texture. We take the first sip of a smoothie with our eyes, and only hard-core addicts thrill to a rhapsody in brown. Experimenting with thousands of combinations, I've developed a set of strategies for healthy, creamy, or frosty smoothies that look gorgeous, taste amazing, and offer big nutritional bang for your buck. Dream up your own blendsations with the Build Your Own Smoothie (page 10) as a guide.

strategies for success

If you've read *The Blender Girl* cookbook, you're probably somewhat familiar with my general smoothie tips. But even so, don't skip this section. There's lots of additional information here (and in The Smoothie Pantry, page 219) that I didn't have space for in the smoothies chapter of that book.

follow the smooth order

For the most efficient blend (and the smoothest consistency), pour liquids into the container first. This helps the blades get moving when you turn on your blender, and encourages the solid ingredients to liquefy more evenly. Next, add powdered ingredients such as cacao, protein blends, and superfood powders, and cover them with soft ingredients like bananas, avocados, fresh berries, and cucumber. (This keeps the powders from flying up into the lid.) After that, throw in hard ingredients like frozen fruits and raw fibrous vegetables. Always throw the ice in last, to help the machine pull all the other ingredients down into the blades for even mixing.

Note: With personal blenders (since you fill, and then invert the container onto the motor to blend), reverse this order and put ice in first.

choose premium produce

Using locally grown organic fruits, vegetables, and herbs in season and at the peak of ripeness supports your local community and gives you flavor-rich blends that are healthy and free of synthetic pesticides and genetic modification. That said, organic produce can be expensive. A good way to compromise is to focus on the produce that's most susceptible to pesticides. Use the Environmental Working Group's "Dirty Dozen" list as your guide for buying organic versions of these: organic leafy greens, berries, broccoli, apples, bell peppers, grapes, kiwis, peaches, nectarines, and celery.

Earthbound Farm (see page 243) is my pick for wonderful store-bought organic leafy greens and frozen fruits and vegetables, and Melissa's Produce (see page 243) ships high-quality organic and conventional fruits and vegetables within the United States. However, your best choice is to grow your own. You don't have to plant a whole garden—growing herbs is easy, even in a small space.

buy fresh, keep fresh

Storing foods properly maximizes longevity, freshness, and flavor. Bananas, citrus, kiwis, tomatoes, pears, and whole mangoes, papayas, and melons are best kept on the counter at room temperature. Once they're peeled and sliced, they should go into the fridge in sealed containers. Apples, berries, and stone fruits (peaches, apricots, plums, cherries, and nectarines) fare better in the fridge. Allow your avocados to ripen at room temperature, but put them in the fridge to slow their ripening or to keep them at their prime longer. Raw nuts and seeds, as well as cold-pressed oils (except olive and coconut), are best stored cold. Superfoods and protein powders, once their packages are opened, keep better chilled, too.

wash your produce thoroughly

Fruits and vegetables can carry soil, bacteria, and pesticide residue, and should be cleaned just prior to using. (Washing in advance is a quick road to rapid rot.) Use a vegetable brush, and rinse under cold water. I wash all produce with a solution of 1 tablespoon of baking soda plus 1 tablespoon of apple cider vinegar or lemon juice per quart (liter) of water, and then rinse well. You can peel foods with edible skins, but much of the goodness in those fruits and veggies is in the skins or just beneath. These recipes only specify peeling (usually of beets, sweet potatoes, or kiwis) when skins would bring down the taste or texture.

use a variety of ingredients

In these smoothies, I've used a range of fresh and frozen fruits for flavor, texture, color, and nutritional variety. I freeze, stew, or dehydrate produce that has been picked at the peak of ripeness and flavor for year-round use. Dried apricots and pears, and unsweetened pear and apricot purees add enormous flavor to smoothies. So do pumpkin butter and applesauce.

freeze your fruit

Fresh, ripe, seasonal fruit adds exquisite flavor to smoothies. But some fruits I use frozen even when they're in season, for a slushy or creamy consistency and ultimate chill factor. Frozen fruit thickens smoothies, and reduces the need for plain ice, which waters down flavor. Frozen fruit is convenient, too, and allows you to enjoy favorites year-round. Buying fruit in season and freezing it will generally save money as well.

add vegetables—as you like them

Vegetables of various kinds work into smoothies with great success—raw, steamed, and roasted. Don't rule out raw veggies frozen, either—our taste buds are temperature sensitive, so frozen produce is milder in flavor. (In small quantities, you won't even taste most things.) Vegetables that are best used fresh are leafy greens, carrots, onions, peas, and fruits we often consider vegetables, such as cucumbers, tomatoes, and avocados. My frozen raw picks: cauliflower, broccoli, peas, spinach, and carrots; those good steamed include carrots and cauliflower; good roasted or steamed are sweet potatoes, pumpkin, squash, and beets.

go savory

Fruit smoothies are delicious. But to reduce sugar spikes, I recommend a moderate intake of these sweet treats and a higher consumption of vegetable blends containing leafy greens and a small amount of apple and lemon. The complex carbohydrates contained in these alkaline, gazpacho-style smoothies are more slowly absorbed and metabolized than the sugars in fruits and can be super tasty. If you prefer to ease into these savory blends, tone down the sugar rush in fruit-based smoothies by adding a cup (or more) of spinach or romaine. These mild-flavored greens boost goodness and blend in virtually undetected. A pinch of natural salt or 1/4 teaspoon of apple cider vinegar helps to balance the acidity of fruit sugars, too.

grate, mince, and zest hard ingredients

Hard ingredients measure with greater accuracy and incorporate most easily into smoothies if they're finely minced or grated. For ginger and horseradish, you'll get the best results with a porcelain ginger grater or a Microplane grater. Kitchen IQ (see page 242) makes a fantastic ginger tool that's super quick and easy. With citrus, I use Kitchen IQ's zesters, which have a plastic backing that catches the zest. Alternatively, use a Microplane to grate the zest of lemons, limes, and oranges.

lift with citrus

I often add a whole peeled lime or half a peeled lemon to alkalize blends, add a refreshing zing, or to lift the pungency of leafy greens. A teaspoon (or more) of lemon or lime juice or a pinch (or more) of zest is brilliant for lifting and brightening the flavors in flat blends. With oranges, less is more (with both juice and zest) unless you want a pronounced orange flavor. Alternatively, green apples (typically the variety with the least sugar content) are wonderful for balancing earthy blends and are less assertive than citrus.

savor with salt

I add a pinch (or more) of high-quality salt to boost the flavor and nutrient density and balance the pH of every smoothie. I use Celtic sea salt from Selina Naturally (see page 243), which has superior quality, nutrient density, and flavor. Himalayan crystal salt is also very good. Both of these salts are mineral-rich and harvested (and sold) as they come from the ocean or the earth. These natural salts punch up the flavors of fruits and vegetables. Melon, for example, benefits greatly from a pinch, as do avocado and tomato. Salt is particularly helpful if your fruit isn't quite ripe. Common table salt, which is generally heated to extreme temperatures, then iodized, bleached, processed, and refined, doesn't have the same flavor effects or health benefits. Salt quantities in these recipes are calculated using high-quality natural varieties. If you're using regular table salt, you'll want to start with half the amount and add to taste.

Rich in alkalizing minerals, high-quality natural salts help neutralize the acidity produced by sugar, stimulate the lymphatic system, replenish electrolytes, and help the body access energy. They also fight bacterial infections, combat environmental pollutants and free radical damage, and assist digestion.

push the probiotics

Consuming probiotic-rich foods to replenish stores of healthy bacteria helps to maintain a balanced inner ecology that supports overall health. Probiotics help build mineral-rich alkaline blood, are essential for the assimilation of protein, improve digestion, boost immunity, and are cleansing. Adding probiotics to your smoothies is an easy, tasty way to get your daily dose. I add ½ teaspoon of probiotic powder to any I make for myself. The taste is undetectable, regardless of the blend, and probiotics are a great way to balance the sugar and acid content of fruit. The really potent probiotics that I prefer require refrigeration. I avoid capsules because the gel cap is not easily digestible, but if that's what you use, just break the shell to release the powder. Unsweetened probiotic-rich liquids like kefirs (water, coconut water, or milk varieties), kombucha, or Kevita (see page 243) make wonderful health-promoting additions to shakes, too.

soak ingredients for the smoothest texture

Raw nuts and seeds and raw or cooked grains give creamy texture, but for best results, soak them. A blend of rolled oats and raw cashews, for example, is brilliant in dessert smoothies, giving the feel of pastry.

how to soak ingredients

Soaking raw nuts, seeds, and whole grains neutralizes enzyme inhibitors, unlocks the food's full nutrient potential, makes proteins more available, and activates live enzymes. Hydrated nuts, seeds, and dried fruits liquefy more completely (even in high-speed machines). For the creamiest smoothies, I recommend soaking at room temperature in glass or ceramic containers (unsealed). Covering jars or bowls with a flour-sack cloth or kitchen towel lets the food breathe.

NUTS, SEEDS, AND GRAINS: To soak the quick way, cover with boiling water for 10 minutes. Drain, discard the soaking liquid, and rinse thoroughly. This fast soak softens foods for smoothies, but at high nutritional cost, as heat destroys live enzymes.

To soak the slow way, submerge in a solution of filtered water, salt, and apple cider vinegar or lemon juice. Adding salt and acid helps to accelerate nutrient activation. As a general rule, I use two parts water to one part food, by volume, and add 1/2 teaspoon of salt and 1 teaspoon of lemon juice or vinegar per quart (or liter) of water. Always discard the soaking liquid, as it contains anti-nutrients that are not beneficial for health. There are short-, medium-, and long-soak foods, and the time required varies. For most nuts and grains, 8 to 12 hours of soaking is right. For more information about soaking foods and a chart for specific soak times, check out my first book, *The Blender Girl*.

DATES: To soak the slow way, pit and chop your dried fruit and cover with filtered water or the recipe's base liquid for 30 minutes to 8 hours. Dates don't contain anti-nutrients like nuts, seeds, and grains, so you can utilize the soaking liquid to enhance sweetness and flavor, or drain the liquid and add only the dates. (No need to rinse.) Soak the quick way by covering with boiling water for 10 minutes. (Fresh dates need less soaking.)

OTHER DRIED FRUITS AND VEGETABLES: Soak raisins, apricots, prunes, cherries, blueberries, goji berries, camu berries, mulberries, and sun-dried tomatoes in a container and pour in just enough filtered water (or the recipe's base liquid) to cover. Soak from 15 minutes to 1 hour, then drain or add the soaking liquid, too.

seal and store smartly

When you can't blend up a smoothie to drink immediately, to minimize oxidation and degradation of nutrients and enjoy the best flavor balance, you don't have to skip it, either. We're all busy, and sometimes need to prepare food in advance. Most of these blends fare well for a bit if chilled or frozen. Some leafy greens (like collards) develop an assertive flavor in a blend, so I've indicated in the recipe summaries which shakes aren't so good if stored for later consumption.

To store a smoothie for up to a few hours, transfer the blend to a glass jar, seal, and chill. For consumption within one day, you'll retain the greatest freshness by wrapping the jar in a vacuum-seal pouch, squeezing out the air, then chilling. If that seems a bit extreme, don't sweat it, just chill. To store for longer than a day, it's better to freeze. Fill an airtight glass container three-quarters full (to allow for expansion as the liquid freezes), and keep frozen for no more than 3 weeks. When you're ready to drink it, thaw it partially (there may be some separation), and reblend (or shake) to enjoy.

beat the bloat

Some people experience bloating after drinking a smoothie. This can be due to excessive fruit intake or food-combining sensitivities. For some, combining fruits and vegetables results in digestive problems, while for others it doesn't. Find what works for you. Generally, leafy greens combine well with all foods. However, there are exceptions. If you're feeling bloated, reduce fruits; avoid combining nut milks, nuts, seeds, and grains with fruits; and soak your nuts and seeds (see page 6).

Purchasing and prepping good quality ingredients are important steps toward good smoothies, but the real magic happens in selecting the perfect blend of flavors.

Using Protein Powder

Vanilla and chocolate protein powders figure in these recipes chiefly as boosters. Finding your favorite can be a grab-and-try exercise, or a matter of working up some criteria to narrow down the choices. My go-to is hemp seed, for its high-quality, digestible protein (see page 235), but for diversity I use a variety, and look for organic, raw, sprouted, unsweetened products. Start with 1 tablespoon and add to taste. Heavy additions can leave a powdery mouthfeel and aftertaste, throwing off the balance of other ingredients. That said, protein powders can enhance creaminess and flavor, and mask the murky taste of green powders.

---

six steps to spectacular smoothies

A basic smoothie contains three essential components: liquid, base, and the chill factor (ice, frozen fruit, or chilled liquid). The Pink Cooler (page 18) is a great example of a simple smoothie with just two ingredients. In this blend, watermelon provides the liquid and frozen strawberries combine with the melon to provide the base flavor as well as the chill factor.

step 1: start with a liquid

A 32-ounce (960ml; 2 servings) smoothie typically requires about 2 cups (480ml) of liquid (choose one type or a combination of types, depending on your other ingredients). If your blend contains high-water-content foods like watermelon, cucumber, orange, or other types of melon, you may need little or no liquid.

step 2: choose your base

Add 2 to 3 cups (320 to 480g) of base ingredients to the liquid. Your base can be a single flavor or a combination of several ingredients.

step 3: get creamy or frosty

I think a creamy or frosty texture is a nonnegotiable element of a great smoothie. Select one item (or sometimes two) from the Cream list (page 10) in the quantities specified, then turn to The Smoothie Pantry on page 219 to choose complementary ingredients. If your base ingredients already deliver a creamy or frosty texture (for example, banana, mashed vegetables, or frozen fruits), you may not need to add anything from the Cream list.

step 4: go green

For maximum nutrition and to alkalize blends, I highly recommend adding some leafy greens. The greens section of The Smoothie Pantry will help you incorporate these with great success.

steps 5 and 6: boost your nutrition and add the magic

Boosters and what I call magic ingredients are optional, but they really increase the nutritional profile of any smoothie and amp up the wow factor. You could pick several items each from the Boosters and Magic lists (page 11) and get incredible results. Again, use The Smoothie Pantry as a guide for pairing flavors. Once you've tried the recipes in this book, and used the boosters and magic ingredients suggested, I bet they'll become must-haves for you, too. After all, these aren't six steps to basic smoothies—they're six steps to spectacular smoothies.

smoothies versus juices

There's a place for both juices and smoothies in any healthy lifestyle. I blend every day and juice every week. Smoothies made with whole fruits and vegetables retain all of the nutrients contained in skins, piths, and sometimes seeds, as well as healthy fiber, which slows down the assimilation of sugars, assists with bowel regularity, and helps to bind and eliminate toxins. I recommend juicing for cleansing purposes or during periods of illness. Juicing removes the fiber, which allows for a more gentle digestive process and leaves more energy for detoxification and regeneration. I drink pulped and pulp-free juices, and to empty and strengthen my system, do a one-day juice fast/cleanse every week, plus a three-day cleanse at the beginning of every season.

build your own smoothie

Liquids	Base	Cream
Water or coconut water: 1 to 2 cups (240 to 480ml) Milk: 1 to 2 cups (240 to 480ml) Juice: 1 to 2 cups (240 to 480ml) Herbal or green tea: 1 cup, plus more to taste (240ml) Kefir or kombucha: 1 cup, plus more to taste (240ml) Aloe vera juice: ¼ cup (60ml)	Fruits or vegetables (fresh, frozen, cooked, or dried; 2 to 3 cups (320 to 480g))	Fruit: 1 avocado, banana, or mango; 1 to 2 cups (160 to 320g) frozen mango, pineapple, or peach Coconut: ½ to 1 cup (90 to 180g) raw meat; 1 tablespoon creamed Yogurt: ¼ to ½ cup (60 to 120g) plain coconut or yogurt of your choice Nuts: ¼ to ½ cup (35 to 70g) raw, unsalted cashews, macadamias, or blanched almonds Seeds: ¼ cup (35g) hemp or sunflower seeds Flavored ice: 1 cup (125g) milk ice cubes (see page 223) Nut butters: 1 to 2 tablespoons nut butter (almond, cashew, macadamia, sunflower seed, hazelnut, or pecan) Tofu, oats, and grains: ¼ cup silken tofu (55g), rolled oats (22g), cooked quinoa (150g), or brown rice (150g) Cooked vegetables: ¼ cup to 1 cup (50 to 200g) cooked carrot, sweet potato, squash, pumpkin, or cauliflower

Greens	Boosters	Magic
Mild: 1 to 2 cups (30 to 60g) spinach, romaine, or radish greens	Seeds: 1 teaspoon to 1 tablespoon chia, flax, or hemp seeds	Spices: A pinch to $1/8$ teaspoon clove, cardamom, cayenne, red pepper flakes, turmeric, or curry powder; $1/4$ to 1 teaspoon cinnamon, nutmeg, or ginger
Medium: $1/2$ to 1 cup (30 to 60g) chard, bok choy, collard greens, beet greens, or kale, plus more to taste	Oil: 1 teaspoon to 1 tablespoon avocado, olive, hemp, flax, coconut, pumpkin seed, or macadamia oil	Fresh herbs: $1 1/2$ teaspoons rosemary; 2 tablespoons to $1/4$ cup (10g) parsley, cilantro, basil, or mint
Strong: 2 tablespoons to $1/4$ cup (6g) dandelion greens or arugula	Superfoods: 1 teaspoon to 1 tablespoon açaí, pomegranate, goji, camu, maqui, or maca powder; 1 tablespoon goji berries, maqui berries, or mulberries	Zest: $1/8$ to 1 teaspoon finely grated lemon, lime, or orange zest
Fresh herbs: 2 tablespoons to $1/4$ cup (6g) basil or mint; $1/2$ to 1 cup (20 to 40g) flat-leaf parsley or cilantro	Green powders: $1/4$ to $1/2$ teaspoon spirulina or chlorella powder; $1/2$ to 1 teaspoon wheatgrass powder, plus more to taste	Chocolate: 1 tablespoon to $1/4$ cup (18g) raw cacao or unsweetened cocoa powder
	Protein powder: 1 tablespoon to 1 scoop, plus more to taste	Natural extracts: $1/8$ to 1 teaspoon vanilla, almond, or peppermint extract; $1/8$ to 1 teaspoon rose or orange blossom water
	Frozen vegetables: $1/4$ to $1/2$ cup (25 to 50g) frozen raw cauliflower or broccoli	Sweetener: fruit concentrate, stevia, dates, maple syrup, coconut nectar, yacon syrup, brown rice syrup, or lucuma powder to taste
	Probiotic powder: $1/2$ teaspoon	Salt: A pinch to 1 teaspoon

CHAPTER 2

find your perfect blend

These recipes have been tested extensively with a variety of blenders to ensure that they're accessible and versatile. However, a high-speed blender will give the best texture. To help conventional blenders: soak nuts, oats, seeds, and dates (see page 6); chop fibrous greens; steam or grate carrots, and roast, steam, or grate beets; mince chiles and herbs; and finely grate or mince ginger, horseradish, and citrus zests. With small personal machines, it helps to blend in batches.

Every recipe makes two servings of about 16 ounces (480ml), but yields vary with the sizes of fruits and vegetables and measuring styles.

The recipes are all gluten-free and vegan; however, they've been tested using dairy milk and unsweetened plain or vanilla Greek-style yogurt. For some combinations—like the alchemy of almond milk and other ingredients in Avo-Nana Bread (page 176)—dairy doesn't deliver the same flavor.

These recipes are highly flexible and customizable, ranging from basic and accessible blends to more exotic and complex combinations, designed to satisfy children, novice smoothie-makers, and advanced cooks. With that in mind, they've been developed for particular and varied flavor profiles. That said, there *are* substitutions that work. But with virtually all substitutions, yields vary and so will taste. That's where flavorful boosters can restore balance or swing things in new directions.

substitutions

- Coconut water and filtered water can be used interchangeably, as can raw cacao and unsweetened cocoa. Flavors change slightly.

- When milk is flexible, the recipe notes that. Dairy and other milks can be substituted except in recipes using coconut milk, where coconutty flavor is essential. You can use boxed coconut milk, but you'll typically get the richest flavor with canned.

- Plain or vanilla Greek-style yogurt can be used (and has been tested) in place of vegan yogurt.

- Juices are generally integral to the characters of blends, so changing them may lead to innovations or to flops.

- Where fresh herbs are specified, dried don't work. Nix the funky-tasting ginger and garlic pre-packed in jars, too.

- Fresh lemon and lime juices yield the best results. Nutrition-free bottled kinds taste awful.

- Sweeteners are flexible. An exception is maple syrup, since its distinct flavor defines certain blends.

- Pomegranate juice and goji juice, with highly assertive flavors, don't substitute for the powdered boosters.

- Frozen cauliflower and broccoli, as boosters, should be used unthawed, so their flavors go undetected. When cooked and cooled cauliflower is called for, it should not be frozen.

- Fresh or frozen fruit? Recipes call for both, depending on the desired texture and chill. Fresh and frozen bananas work interchangeably. (Add ice with fresh; with frozen, you may need additional liquid.) If you substitute fresh fruit for frozen, add ice for chill or for creamy or frosty texture. I use frozen mangoes, pineapples, and peaches to thicken and cream-up smoothies; fresh fruit will produce a more watery result. Canned fruit works okay in some blends (particularly those with peaches, apricots, plums, and pears). Choose fruit canned in natural juice (not syrup), rinse, and reduce sweetener to taste.

choosing your recipe

The recipe descriptions call out flavor profiles and nutritional benefits. For quick reference, icons tag recipes by category:

detox	energizing	inflammation
weight loss	protein rich	contains nuts
immunity	alkaline	unsweetened

All of the recipes are gluten-free and vegan (dairy-free and egg-free). In addition to the categories above you'll also find recipes that are paleo, low fat, and low carb listed out in the index.

Following every recipe comes the nutrition breakdown: calories, fat, saturated fats, sodium, carbohydrate, fiber, sugar, protein, calcium, and iron. The stats are for the base recipe (per 16-ounce/480ml serving), and don't factor in boosters.

Use the recipes (and the strategies employed in them) as inspiration to find *your* perfect blend.

how to use the boosters

The three optional boosters featured with each recipe are chosen to enhance flavor and/or nutrition. Boosters give simple blends complex flavor, and each one adds another dimension. To blends bursting with personality, boosters add nutrients and leave flavor alone. The options work separately and together, so you can supplement the base recipe with one, two, or all three.

As the recipes serve two, you can make the basic blend and serve half unboosted to one person, then add options to the second portion (halving the boosters' quantities).

CHAPTER 4

the recipes

You'll marvel that this simple sip can taste so sweet! Stevia enhances the flavors of strawberry and watermelon, as do the ginger and mint boosters. Watermelon's lycopene and citrulline aid cardiovascular health. This hydrating combo has anti-inflammatory agents and antioxidants, too.

SERVES 2

3 ½ cups (560g) chopped seedless watermelon

2 cups (320g) frozen strawberries

OPTIONAL BOOSTERS

1 teaspoon minced ginger, plus more to taste

2 tablespoons chopped mint

1 tablespoon pomegranate powder

Throw all of the ingredients into your blender and blast on high for 30 to 60 seconds, until smooth and creamy.

NUTRITIONAL FACTS (PER SERVING)

CALORIES 135 KCAL | FAT 0 G | SATURATED FAT 0 G | SODIUM 4 MG | CARBS 33 G | FIBER 4 G | SUGARS 25 G
PROTEIN 2 G | CALCIUM 45 MG | IRON 1 MG

pink cooler

INFLAMMATION   DETOX   WEIGHT LOSS   ALKALINE   UNSWEETENED

For a full-flavor adventure, add all three boosters to this simple and sweet immunity blend. Cauliflower delivers extra vitamin C and nutrients, yogurt adds creaminess and probiotic power, and the cardamom kicks the experience into "oh!"

SERVES 2

4 medium oranges, peeled, seeded, and quartered

1 tablespoon coconut nectar or other liquid sweetener

1 cup (160g) frozen peaches

1 cup (125g) ice cubes

OPTIONAL BOOSTERS

¼ cup (60g) plain or vanilla-flavored yogurt

¼ cup (30g) frozen raw cauliflower florets

⅛ teaspoon ground cardamom

Throw all of the ingredients into your blender and blast on high for 30 to 60 seconds, until smooth and creamy.

NUTRITIONAL FACTS (PER SERVING)

CALORIES 184 KCAL | FAT 0 G | SATURATED FAT 0 G | SODIUM 2 MG | CARBS 46 G | FIBER 8 G | SUGARS 38 G
PROTEIN 3 G | CALCIUM 111 MG | IRON 0 MG

orange o

ENERGIZING   **IMMUNITY**   **DETOX**   **WEIGHT LOSS**

This delicious digestive is also an arthritis ace. The honeydew's water-to-potassium ratio and the basil's vitamin K lower blood pressure, aid muscle and nerve function, and calm the body. The basil eases cramps and bloating, adds anti-inflammatory power, inhibits bacterial growth, and reduces radiation damage.

SERVES 2

4 cups (680g) chopped and chilled ripe honeydew melon

2 tablespoons chopped basil, plus more to taste

2 tablespoons freshly squeezed lemon juice

1/2 small avocado, pitted and peeled

10 drops alcohol-free liquid stevia, plus more to taste

Pinch of natural salt

1 1/2 cups (190g) ice cubes

OPTIONAL BOOSTERS

1/2 teaspoon wheatgrass powder

1 tablespoon chia seeds

1 teaspoon flaxseed oil

Throw all of the ingredients (except the ice cubes) into your blender and blast on high for 30 to 60 seconds, until smooth. Add the ice cubes and blast for 10 to 20 seconds more, until well combined.

NUTRITIONAL FACTS (PER SERVING)

CALORIES 182 KCAL | FAT 5 G | SATURATED FAT 0 G | SODIUM 142 MG | CARBS 34 G | FIBER 5 G | SUGARS 28 G
PROTEIN 2 G | CALCIUM 33 MG | IRON 0 MG

basil melon mania

DETOX

WEIGHT LOSS

UNSWEETENED

ALKALINE

With a creamy texture and exquisite flavor, this immunity blend is fabulous for collagen formation and glowing skin, hair, and nails. Mango's enzymes and vitamins A, C, and E cleanse the liver and aid digestion, and its potassium and fiber help regulate blood pressure and cholesterol. This one will make your heart happy.

SERVES 2

1 1/2 cups (360ml) freshly squeezed orange juice

1/2 cup (120ml) water, plus more as needed

1/2 medium avocado, pitted and peeled

1/2 teaspoon finely grated lime zest

1/8 teaspoon ground cardamom

2 cups (320g) frozen mango

1/2 cup (62g) ice cubes

OPTIONAL BOOSTERS

1/2 teaspoon wheatgrass powder

1 teaspoon chia seeds

1 teaspoon flaxseed oil

Throw all of the ingredients into your blender and blast on high for 30 to 60 seconds, until smooth and creamy. Add more water as needed to blend.

NUTRITIONAL FACTS (PER SERVING)

CALORIES 260 KCAL | FAT 8 G | SATURATED FAT 1 G | SODIUM 10 MG | CARBS 47 G | FIBER 6 G | SUGARS 37 G
PROTEIN 3 G | CALCIUM 47 MG | IRON 0 MG

mystical mango

ENERGIZING   IMMUNITY   DETOX   UNSWEETENED

This low-fat, high–vitamin C blend is great for weight loss, fighting infection, and scavenging free radicals. The anti-inflammatory lupeol and fisetin in strawberries neutralize colon, cervical, and breast cancer cells, and with the lycopene in red grapefruit, this blend has prostate health covered, too. The ginger booster adds an amazing zing.

SERVES 2

2 ¼ cups (540ml) unsweetened grapefruit juice

¼ cup (60ml) water, plus more as needed

3 cups (480g) frozen strawberries

5 drops alcohol-free liquid stevia, plus more to taste

OPTIONAL BOOSTERS

1 teaspoon minced ginger

1 tablespoon chia seeds

1 tablespoon pomegranate powder

Throw all of the ingredients into your blender and blast on high for 30 to 60 seconds, until smooth and creamy. Add more water as needed to blend. Tweak sweetener to taste.

NUTRITIONAL FACTS (PER SERVING)

CALORIES 187 KCAL | FAT 0 G | SATURATED FAT 0 G | SODIUM 6 MG | CARBS 43 G | FIBER 5 G | SUGARS 37 G
PROTEIN 2 G | CALCIUM 64 MG | IRON 1 MG

grapefruit-straw

INFLAMMATION DETOX WEIGHT LOSS ALKALINE

Pineapple, kiwi, and basil are a magical flavor combo. Bromelain and flavonoids join with blood-pressure-regulating omega-3s, lutein, and manganese to reduce inflammation, promote heart health, combat aging, and boost metabolism and digestion. High vitamin C levels and antibacterial potential make this a cold-and-flu buster, too.

SERVES 2

1¾ cups (420ml) freshly squeezed orange juice

4 medium kiwis, peeled and chopped

¼ cup (11g) firmly packed basil

2½ cups (450g) frozen pineapple

OPTIONAL BOOSTERS

1 cup (25g) torn-up curly green kale (1 or 2 large leaves with stalk removed)

1 teaspoon wheatgrass powder

1 teaspoon avocado oil

Throw all of the ingredients into your blender and blast on high for 30 to 60 seconds, until smooth and creamy.

NUTRITIONAL FACTS (PER SERVING)

CALORIES 295 KCAL | FAT 1 G | SATURATED FAT 0 G | SODIUM 8 MG | CARBS 72 G | FIBER 7 G | SUGARS 52 G
PROTEIN 4 G | CALCIUM 109 MG | IRON 1 MG

pineapple kiwi cavalcade

INFLAMMATION   IMMUNITY   DETOX   UNSWEETENED

Vitamins A and C, potassium, and flavonoids in apricots are potent health promoters that combat macular degeneration and regulate heart rate and blood pressure. Apricots alleviate menstrual cramps, and their lycopenes promote prostate health. Don't skip the boosters—protein powder adds creaminess, and cardamom takes this blend from simple to spectacular.

SERVES 2

1½ cups (360ml) coconut water or water

4 medium apricots, pitted and chopped

1 teaspoon coconut nectar or pure maple syrup, plus more to taste

2 cups (320g) frozen peaches

OPTIONAL BOOSTERS

⅛ teaspoon ground cardamom

1 teaspoon camu powder

1 tablespoon vanilla protein powder

Throw all of the ingredients into your blender and blast on high for 30 to 60 seconds, until smooth and creamy. Tweak sweetener to taste.

NUTRITIONAL FACTS (PER SERVING)

CALORIES 104 KCAL | FAT 0 G | SATURATED FAT 0 G | SODIUM 8 MG | CARBS 25 G | FIBER 3 G | SUGARS 21 G | PROTEIN 2 G | CALCIUM 27 MG | IRON 0 MG

apricot ammunition

IMMUNITY   DETOX   WEIGHT LOSS

Plums can be stifled in smoothies, but here the ripe fruit sings, with ginger and maple providing backup. This high-fiber blend is a brilliant digestive aid: sorbitol and isatin work as natural laxatives, promoting regularity and alleviating constipation. Or forget all that and just enjoy the incredible flavor.

SERVES 2

½ cup (120ml) coconut water

4 medium red or black plums, pitted and roughly chopped

1 tablespoon pure maple syrup

1 teaspoon minced ginger

1 cup (160g) frozen raspberries

1 cup (125g) ice cubes

OPTIONAL BOOSTERS

¼ cup (30g) frozen raw cauliflower florets

2 teaspoons maqui powder

1 tablespoon chia seeds

Throw all of the ingredients into your blender and blast on high for 30 to 60 seconds, until smooth and creamy.

NUTRITIONAL FACTS (PER SERVING)

CALORIES 140 KCAL | FAT 1 G | SATURATED FAT 0 G | SODIUM 67 MG | CARBS 33 G | FIBER 7 G | SUGARS 24 G
PROTEIN 2 G | CALCIUM 54 MG | IRON 0 MG

plum potion

ENERGIZING   IMMUNITY

Loaded with vitamin C, this delicious blend is a powerful cold and flu fighter. Vitamin A helps to maintain healthy mucous membranes, and the bromelain (an enzyme in pineapple) reduces inflammation and helps to suppress coughs and loosen mucus. Add the dandelion greens for an exotic ride.

SERVES 2

½ cup (120ml) coconut water or water

2 oranges, peeled, seeded, and quartered

1 green apple, skin on, cored and chopped

1½ cups (240g) frozen pineapple

OPTIONAL BOOSTERS

¼ (3g) cup loosely packed dandelion greens

1 tablespoon raw unsalted cashews, soaked (see page 6)

1 tablespoon pomegranate powder

Throw all of the ingredients into your blender and blast on high for 30 to 60 seconds, until smooth and creamy.

NUTRITIONAL FACTS (PER SERVING)

CALORIES 193 KCAL | FAT 0 G | SATURATED FAT 0 G | SODIUM 4 MG | CARBS 49 G | FIBER 8 G | SUGARS 38 G
PROTEIN 2 G | CALCIUM 96 MG | IRON 0 MG

fruity fun

IMMUNITY   DETOX   WEIGHT LOSS   UNSWEETENED

This divine refresher makes skin sing. Nectarines contain bioflavonoids, antioxidants, and vitamin C that stimulate collagen synthesis and shield against UV damage. For expectant mothers, folate and potassium foster healthy baby growth, prevent muscle cramps, and boost energy. Add ginger and cayenne, and salt the rim of your glass for mocktail magic.

SERVES 2

1 cup (240ml) coconut water

2 ripe nectarines, pitted and chopped

1½ tablespoons freshly squeezed lemon juice, plus more to taste

1 cup (160g) frozen peaches

1 cup (125g) ice cubes

Natural sweetener to taste (optional)

OPTIONAL BOOSTERS

Tiny pinch of cayenne pepper

1 teaspoon minced ginger

¼ cup (30g) frozen raw cauliflower florets

Throw all of the ingredients into your blender and blast on high for 30 to 60 seconds, until smooth and creamy.

NUTRITIONAL FACTS (PER SERVING)

CALORIES 118 KCAL | FAT 0 G | SATURATED FAT 0 G | SODIUM 128 MG | CARBS 27 G | FIBER 4 G | SUGARS 21 G PROTEIN 3 G | CALCIUM 44 MG | IRON 0 MG

nectarita

IMMUNITY   DETOX   WEIGHT LOSS   UNSWEETENED

High in vitamin C and fiber, this immunity blend is an anti-cancer avenger. The anthocyanin pigments in blackberries combine with the flavonoids in basil for an anti-inflammatory punch, protecting cells from oxidation and chromosomes from radiation. An antibacterial superstar, basil also eases cramps, bloating, and indigestion. Add the orange blossom water for a "wow!"

SERVES 2

1 cup (240ml) coconut water or water, plus more as needed

1 cup (240ml) freshly squeezed orange juice

3 cups (480g) frozen blackberries

1/2 cup (80g) frozen mango

1/2 cup (14g) loosely packed chopped basil, plus more to taste

OPTIONAL BOOSTERS

1 tablespoon maqui powder

1/4 cup (30g) frozen raw broccoli florets

1/8 teaspoon pure orange blossom water

Throw all of the ingredients into your blender and blast on high for 30 to 60 seconds, until smooth and creamy. Add more coconut water as needed to blend. Tweak basil to taste.

NUTRITIONAL FACTS (PER SERVING)

CALORIES 185 KCAL | FAT 1 G | SATURATED FAT 0 G | SODIUM 9 MG | CARBS 42 G | FIBER 13 G | SUGARS 27 G
PROTEIN 4 G | CALCIUM 109 MG | IRON 2 MG

black magic

 INFLAMMATION   IMMUNITY   DETOX   WEIGHT LOSS   UNSWEETENED

This sensational tropical trip delivers ultimate potassium power to normalize blood pressure and maintain fluid and electrolyte balance, which contributes to kidney health. Peaches, apricots, and bananas deliver a healthy dose, as do all three boosters. A nip of rum transforms this into a cocktail with kick.

SERVES 2

1½ cups (360g) coconut water or water

2 medium apricots, pitted and chopped

1 medium sliced banana, fresh or frozen

1 tablespoon creamed coconut

2 teaspoons freshly squeezed lemon juice

1½ cups (240g) frozen peaches

OPTIONAL BOOSTERS

¼ cup (30g) frozen raw broccoli florets

½ cup (15g) loosely packed chard leaves

2 raw Brazil nuts

Throw all of the ingredients into your blender and blast on high for about 1 minute, until smooth and creamy.

NUTRITIONAL FACTS (PER SERVING)

CALORIES 129 KCAL | FAT 1 G | SATURATED FAT 1 G | SODIUM 8 MG | CARBS 29 G | FIBER 4 G | SUGARS 20 G PROTEIN 2 G | CALCIUM 20 MG | IRON 0 MG

potassium plus

ENERGIZING **IMMUNITY** **WEIGHT LOSS** **UNSWEETENED**

This blend will transport you to tropical paradise (don't skip the chile). Loaded with vitamins A and C, fiber, manganese, and enzymes (papaya's papain and pineapple's bromelain), this cleansing cocktail aids digestion and alleviates bloating. The anti-inflammatory power can support recovery from sports injuries and other physical trauma.

SERVES 2

1 cup (240ml) canned coconut milk (shake, then pour)

¼ cup (60ml) freshly squeezed orange juice

1½ cups (240g) chopped papaya

1 tablespoon coconut nectar or other liquid sweetener

Pinch of finely grated orange zest

¾ cup (120g) frozen pineapple

¾ cup (120g) frozen strawberries

1 cup (125g) ice cubes

OPTIONAL BOOSTERS

1 tablespoon coconut oil

1 tablespoon pomegranate powder

½ teaspoon finely chopped serrano chile, plus more to taste

Throw all of the ingredients into your blender and blast on high for about 1 minute, until smooth and creamy.

NUTRITIONAL FACTS (PER SERVING)

Calories 367 kcal | Fat 24 g | Saturated fat 21 g | Sodium 28 mg | Carbs 39 g | Fiber 4 g | Sugars 28 g | Protein 3 g | Calcium 67 mg | Iron 4 mg

pine-papaya-yay!

INFLAMMATION   ENERGIZING   IMMUNITY

With a little sweetness and the zing of ginger (add mint for a "wow" factor), this hydrating and cleansing blend is loaded with vitamins A and C—great for immunity and cell regeneration, skin tone, and vision. Plus, the melon's potassium helps regulate blood pressure and protect against stroke and heart disease.

SERVES 2

½ cup (120ml) freshly squeezed orange juice

1½ cups (225g) chilled chopped cantaloupe

1½ cups (225g) chilled chopped honeydew melon

1 orange, peeled, seeded, and quartered

1 teaspoon minced ginger

½ small avocado, pitted and peeled

Pinch of natural salt

5 drops alcohol-free liquid stevia, plus more to taste

1 cup (125g) ice cubes

OPTIONAL BOOSTERS

2 tablespoons chopped mint

1 teaspoon pomegranate powder

1 teaspoon flaxseed oil

Throw all of the ingredients (except the ice cubes) into your blender and blast on high for 30 to 60 seconds, until smooth and creamy. Add the ice and blend for a few seconds more, until smooth and chilled.

NUTRITIONAL FACTS (PER SERVING)

CALORIES 206 KCAL | FAT 5 G | SATURATED FAT 0 G | SODIUM 118 MG | CARBS 39 G | FIBER 6 G | SUGARS 32 G
PROTEIN 3 G | CALCIUM 66 MG | IRON 0 MG

melon ball

INFLAMMATION   IMMUNITY   DETOX   ALKALINE   UNSWEETENED

This blend is sweet and tangy, with beautiful, warming notes of ginger. The tofu creates an amazing, creamy texture, and with the chia seeds and almond milk, delivers a healthy dose of plant-based calcium for strong bones. Add all three boosters for more calcium karma.

SERVES 2

1 cup (240ml) freshly squeezed orange juice

1 cup (240ml) unsweetened almond milk or other nut, grain, or seed milk (strained if homemade)

½ cup (110g) silken tofu

1 tablespoon chia seeds

1 teaspoon freshly squeezed lemon juice

1½ teaspoons minced ginger

1½ cups (240g) frozen raspberries

1 cup (160g) frozen pineapple

5 drops alcohol-free liquid stevia, plus more to taste

OPTIONAL BOOSTERS

¼ cup (30g) frozen raw broccoli florets

¼ cup (30g) frozen raw cauliflower florets

1 teaspoon ground flaxseeds

Throw all of the ingredients into your blender and blast on high for about 1 minute, until smooth and creamy.

NUTRITIONAL FACTS (PER SERVING)

CALORIES 243 KCAL | FAT 5 G | SATURATED FAT 0 G | SODIUM 85 MG | CARBS 44 G | FIBER 11 G | SUGARS 27 G PROTEIN 7 G | CALCIUM 398 MG | IRON 2 MG

crimson karma

PROTEIN RICH   ENERGIZING   IMMUNITY   UNSWEETENED

These fruit flavors parade across the palate, providing essential vitamins and minerals, fiber, antioxidants, and phenolics to strengthen immunity; promote nerve and cell function; improve cardiovascular, digestive, and eye health; and boost metabolism. A bit of lime zest brightens the flavor, and arugula adds a peppery note.

SERVES 2

1 cup (240ml) coconut water or water

1 ripe medium plum, pitted and chopped

1 ripe medium nectarine, pitted and chopped

1 ripe medium apricot, pitted and chopped

Pinch of natural salt (optional, to bring out flavors)

Pinch of finely grated lime zest (optional)

1½ cups (240g) frozen peaches

½ cup (62g) ice cubes

OPTIONAL BOOSTERS

1 tablespoon pomegranate powder

2 tablespoons (3g) loosely packed arugula

1 teaspoon hemp oil

Throw all of the ingredients (except the frozen peaches and ice cubes) into your blender and blast on high for about 30 seconds, until well combined. Throw in the frozen peaches and ice cubes and blend on high for 10 to 20 seconds more, until chilled and creamy.

NUTRITIONAL FACTS (PER SERVING)

CALORIES 101 KCAL | FAT 0 G | SATURATED FAT 0 G | SODIUM 80 MG | CARBS 24 G | FIBER 3 G | SUGARS 20 G
PROTEIN 2 G | CALCIUM 20 MG | IRON 0 MG

summer stoner

ENERGIZING   DETOX   WEIGHT LOSS   UNSWEETENED

This exotic blend sips like a fancy cocktail, but skips the hefty bar tab. Melon is hydrating, and rich in vitamin C and anti-inflammatory lycopenes, while rosemary contributes awesome flavor and antibacterial backup. The combination makes this your secret immunity agent! Throw in the jalapeño for an added cleanse and kick.

SERVES 2

3 cups (480g) chopped seedless watermelon, chilled

1 teaspoon finely grated lemon zest

1 lemon, peeled and seeded

1½ teaspoons finely chopped rosemary

½ cup (80g) frozen pineapple

¼ cup (80g) frozen strawberries

5 drops alcohol-free liquid stevia, plus more to taste (optional)

OPTIONAL BOOSTERS

½ cup (60g) frozen raw cauliflower florets

½ teaspoon cold-pressed, extra-virgin olive oil

¼ teaspoon finely chopped jalapeño chile

Throw all of the ingredients into your blender and blast on high for 30 to 60 seconds, until well combined.

NUTRITIONAL FACTS (PER SERVING)

CALORIES 115 KCAL | FAT 0 G | SATURATED FAT 0 G | SODIUM 4 MG | CARBS 29 G | FIBER 3 G | SUGARS 21 G
PROTEIN 2 G | CALCIUM 42 MG | IRON 1 MG

rosemary melonade

INFLAMMATION DETOX WEIGHT LOSS UNSWEETENED

Delivering heart health and flavor reminiscent of cranberry sauce, the ginger and cinnamon make this a multidimensional experience. Add a tiny pinch of ground cloves for an added layer of flavor. Cranberries and oranges provide an army of phytonutrients that pack an anti-inflammatory punch, prevent thickening of arteries, regulate blood pressure, and reduce LDL cholesterol, while vitamins A and C promote immunity and glowing skin.

SERVES 2

1 cup (240ml) freshly squeezed orange juice

1 cup (240ml) water

2 medium oranges, peeled, seeded, and quartered

½ small avocado, pitted and peeled

¼ teaspoon finely grated orange zest

2 cups (240g) frozen cranberries

10 drops alcohol-free liquid stevia or 1 tablespoon pure maple syrup, plus more to taste

OPTIONAL BOOSTERS

1 teaspoon minced ginger, plus more to taste

¼ teaspoon ground cinnamon

1 tablespoon chia seeds

Throw all of the ingredients into your blender and blast on high for about 1 minute, until smooth and creamy. Tweak sweetener to taste.

NUTRITIONAL FACTS (PER SERVING)

CALORIES 255 KCAL | FAT 5 G | SATURATED FAT 0 G | SODIUM 12 MG | CARBS 52 G | FIBER 11 G | SUGARS 33 G
PROTEIN 3 G | CALCIUM 94 MG | IRON 0 MG

cran-orange crave

INFLAMMATION　　IMMUNITY　　DETOX　　ALKALINE　　UNSWEETENED

This hydrating helper is a headache remedy and skin and stomach soother. Vitamins A, C, and E in melon encourage cell regeneration, and the mint and ginger settle the stomach and calm the nervous system. Ripe, chilled melon and the pinch of salt are essential.

SERVES 2

½ cup (120ml) coconut water or water

3 ½ cups (595g) chilled chopped honeydew melon

2 tablespoons freshly squeezed lemon juice

½ cup (18g) firmly packed mint

½ small avocado, pitted and peeled

Pinch of natural salt, plus more to taste

10 drops alcohol-free liquid stevia, plus more to taste

1½ cups (190g) ice cubes

OPTIONAL BOOSTERS

1 teaspoon minced ginger

1 teaspoon flaxseed oil

½ teaspoon wheatgrass powder

Throw all of the ingredients into your blender and blast on high for 30 to 60 seconds, until smooth and creamy.

NUTRITIONAL FACTS (PER SERVING)

CALORIES 168 KCAL | FAT 5 G | SATURATED FAT 0 G | SODIUM 138 MG | CARBS 31 G | FIBER 5 G | SUGARS 24 G PROTEIN 2 G | CALCIUM 35 MG | IRON 1 MG

honeydewy skin

DETOX   WEIGHT LOSS   UNSWEETENED   ALKALINE

With ripe melon, this hydrating, probiotic-rich blend tastes like a Creamsicle. Cantaloupe has some of the highest levels of vitamin A, and the flavonoids beta-carotene, lutein, and zeaxanthin can boost vision and protect against macular degeneration. Tweak the orange juice and stevia to taste.

SERVES 2

½ cup (120ml) freshly squeezed orange juice

3 cups (450g) chilled chopped cantaloupe

½ cup (120g) plain or vanilla-flavored yogurt

1 teaspoon freshly squeezed lime juice

½ medium frozen sliced banana

½ cup (62g) ice cubes

OPTIONAL BOOSTERS

Pinch of finely grated lemon zest

1 tablespoon chia seeds

1 tablespoon goji powder

Throw all of the ingredients into your blender and blast on high for 30 to 60 seconds, until smooth and creamy.

NUTRITIONAL FACTS (PER SERVING)

CALORIES 167 KCAL | FAT 2 G | SATURATED FAT 1 G | SODIUM 65 MG | CARBS 34 G | FIBER 2 G | SUGARS 29 G
PROTEIN 4 G | CALCIUM 102 MG | IRON 0 MG

crazy for cantaloupe

ENERGIZING   IMMUNITY   DETOX   UNSWEETENED

This simple blend has a delightful sweetness. Rich in folate (which is great for pregnant women), tangerines help build healthy DNA and red blood cells. Loaded with phytonutrients and vitamins A, C, and E, both mangoes and tangerines boost immunity, strengthen vision, and promote healthy skin, hair, and bones.

SERVES 2

1¾ cups (420ml) unsweetened tangerine juice

3 tangerines or mandarin oranges, peeled and seeded

1 tablespoon freshly squeezed lime juice

1½ cups (240g) frozen mango

OPTIONAL BOOSTERS

1 teaspoon camu powder

1 teaspoon hemp oil

1 teaspoon ground flaxseeds

Throw all of the ingredients into your blender and blast on high for about 1 minute, until smooth and creamy.

NUTRITIONAL FACTS (PER SERVING)

Calories 166 kcal | Fat 0 g | Saturated fat 0 g | Sodium 3 mg | Carbs 40 g | Fiber 2 g | Sugars 37 g Protein 2 g | Calcium 53 mg | Iron 0 mg

tangerine tango

ENERGIZING IMMUNITY DETOX UNSWEETENED

So simple and so delicious, this low-fat, high-fiber cleansing quencher screams vitamin C! A host of phytonutrients makes it an anti-inflammatory, heart-healthy superstar. The lycopene in watermelon, phenolic compounds in raspberries, and flavonoids in basil protect cells against oxygen damage, maintain healthy bones, and regulate cholesterol.

SERVES 2

3 1/2 cups (560g) chopped seedless watermelon

2 cups (320g) frozen raspberries

1/4 cup (7g) loosely packed basil

Natural sweetener to taste (optional)

OPTIONAL BOOSTERS

1 teaspoon pomegranate powder

1/4 cup (30g) frozen raw cauliflower florets

1 tablespoon chia seeds

Throw all of the ingredients into your blender and blast on high for about 1 minute, until smooth and creamy. Tweak sweetener to taste.

NUTRITIONAL FACTS (PER SERVING)

CALORIES 168 KCAL | FAT 1 G | SATURATED FAT 0 G | SODIUM 4 MG | CARBS 40 G | FIBER 11 G | SUGARS 24 G PROTEIN 3 G | CALCIUM 65 MG | IRON 1 MG

happy hydration

INFLAMMATION

IMMUNITY

DETOX

WEIGHT LOSS

UNSWEETENED

This powerful anti-inflammatory, detox, and immunity blend is sweet and rich in antioxidants. Vitamins A and C fight infection, maintain healthy mucus membranes and skin, and preserve vision. The potassium in the orange juice and flesh regulates heart rate and blood pressure, the lycopenes in red grapefruit promote prostate health, and the arugula booster adds a peppery note.

SERVES 2

1 cup (240ml) freshly squeezed orange juice

1 medium red grapefruit, peel and pith removed, seeded, and cut into chunks

1 orange, peeled and segmented

½ small avocado, pitted and peeled

5 drops alcohol-free liquid stevia, plus more to taste

1 cup (125g) ice cubes

OPTIONAL BOOSTERS

1 teaspoon goji powder

1 teaspoon minced ginger

¼ cup (7g) firmly packed arugula

Throw all of the ingredients (except the ice cubes) into your blender and blast on high for about 30 seconds, until smooth and creamy. Add the ice and blast for a few seconds more, until smooth and chilled.

NUTRITIONAL FACTS (PER SERVING)

CALORIES 206 KCAL | FAT 5 G | SATURATED FAT 0 G | SODIUM 6 MG | CARBS 39 G | FIBER 6 G | SUGARS 27 G PROTEIN 3 G | CALCIUM 83 MG | IRON 0 MG

morning sunshine

INFLAMMATION   IMMUNITY   DETOX   UNSWEETENED

With crazy antioxidant levels (the boosters ramp them up even more), this tart, refreshing blend aids immunity, reduces inflammation, and regulates blood pressure and cholesterol. The grapefruit's lycopene combats UV damage—reducing the risk of skin cancer—and is a pal to the prostate. Heart-healthy and cancer-crushing, this blender blast will keep you fighting.

SERVES 2

1 cup (240ml) unsweetened pomegranate juice

½ medium red grapefruit, peel and pith removed, seeded, and cut into chunks

1 green apple, skin on, cored and chopped

5 drops alcohol-free liquid stevia, plus more to taste

¾ cup (120g) frozen pineapple

OPTIONAL BOOSTERS

1 teaspoon camu powder

1 tablespoon chia seeds

¼ cup (30g) frozen raw cauliflower florets

Throw all of the ingredients (except the frozen pineapple) into your blender and blast on high for 30 to 60 seconds, until pureed. Add the frozen pineapple and blend for 10 to 20 seconds more, until smooth.

NUTRITIONAL FACTS (PER SERVING)

CALORIES 170 KCAL | FAT 0 G | SATURATED FAT 0 G | SODIUM 12 MG | CARBS 43 G | FIBER 4 G | SUGARS 35 G
PROTEIN 1 G | CALCIUM 40 MG | IRON 0 MG

the warrior

INFLAMMATION IMMUNITY DETOX ALKALINE UNSWEETENED

Hydrating, cleansing, and energizing, the flavor of this dimensional blend explodes in the mouth (add the cayenne) and kick-starts metabolism while replenishing minerals and vitamins scared off by alcohol. Antioxidants in strawberries reduce damage to the stomach lining, the quercetin in apple skins protects brain cells, and cranberries foster intestinal balance.

SERVES 2

1 1/2 cups (360ml) unfiltered apple juice

1/2 cup (120ml) unsweetened cranberry juice

2 cups (320g) frozen strawberries

1/2 cup (80g) frozen mango

1 teaspoon minced ginger

OPTIONAL BOOSTERS

1 cup (27g) loosely packed baby spinach

1 teaspoon camu powder

Pinch of cayenne pepper

Throw all of the ingredients into your blender and blast on high for 30 to 60 seconds, until smooth and creamy.

NUTRITIONAL FACTS (PER SERVING)

CALORIES 190 KCAL | FAT 0 G | SATURATED FAT 0 G | SODIUM 10 MG | CARBS 47 G | FIBER 4 G | SUGARS 38 G PROTEIN 1 G | CALCIUM 50 MG | IRON 1 MG

hangover helper

IMMUNITY   DETOX   WEIGHT LOSS   UNSWEETENED

This combination is light and zesty. Add ginger for extra zing. Rich in vitamins A, C, E, and K and antioxidants, this blend purifies the blood. It's also wonderful for bone and dental health (the eugenol in parsley is a natural gum-protecting antiseptic).

SERVES 2

½ cup (120ml) freshly squeezed lemon juice

3 cups (510g) green seedless grapes

1 bunch flat-leaf parsley, chopped

½ small avocado, pitted and peeled

5 drops alcohol-free liquid stevia, plus more to taste

2 cups (250g) ice cubes

OPTIONAL BOOSTERS

2 teaspoons minced ginger, plus more to taste

1 teaspoon flaxseed oil

½ teaspoon wheatgrass powder

Throw all of the ingredients into your blender and blast on high for 30 to 60 seconds, until smooth.

NUTRITIONAL FACTS (PER SERVING)

CALORIES 256 KCAL | FAT 5 G | SATURATED FAT 0 G | SODIUM 29 MG | CARBS 55 G | FIBER 5 G | SUGARS 41 G
PROTEIN 3 G | CALCIUM 78 MG | IRON 3 MG

grape-parsley lemonade

 INFLAMMATION IMMUNITY DETOX UNSWEETENED

In this dessert-style green smoothie, the alchemy of ripe peach, mango, almond milk, and maple conjures up the flavor of caramel. Amp up the effect with lucuma powder, which is rich in vitamins A and C, and great for boosting immunity and vision.

SERVES 2

2 cups (480ml) unsweetened almond milk or other nut, grain, or seed milk (strained if homemade)

½ medium sliced banana, fresh or frozen

2 cups (86g) firmly packed baby spinach

1 teaspoon natural vanilla extract

1 tablespoon pure maple syrup or coconut nectar, plus more to taste

1 cup (160g) frozen mango

1 cup (160g) frozen peaches

OPTIONAL BOOSTERS

1 tablespoon chia seeds

1 tablespoon flaxseed oil

2 teaspoons lucuma powder

Throw all of the ingredients into your blender and blast on high for 30 to 60 seconds, until smooth and creamy.

NUTRITIONAL FACTS (PER SERVING)

CALORIES 207 KCAL | FAT 3 G | SATURATED FAT 0 G | SODIUM 187 MG | CARBS 42 G | FIBER 5 G | SUGARS 34 G PROTEIN 3 G | CALCIUM 519 MG | IRON 2 MG

creamy dreamy

ENERGIZING

IMMUNITY

High in fiber and phytonutrients, raspberries stabilize blood sugar and boost fat metabolism, making this vibrant, tangy refresher a weight-loss machine. Radish greens deliver vitamin C, protein, and calcium, and the antioxidant and anti-inflammatory phytonutrients in the berries inhibit abnormal cell division to combat cancer growth.

SERVES 2

2 cups (480ml) coconut water or water

1 cup (37g) loosely packed radish greens

2 cups (320g) frozen raspberries

1/2 cup (80g) frozen mango

5 drops alcohol-free liquid stevia, plus more to taste

OPTIONAL BOOSTERS

1 tablespoon chopped mint

1 tablespoon maqui powder

1/4 cup (30g) frozen raw cauliflower florets

Throw all of the ingredients into your blender and blast on high for 30 to 60 seconds, until smooth and creamy. Tweak sweetener to taste.

NUTRITIONAL FACTS (PER SERVING)

CALORIES 109 KCAL | FAT 1 G | SATURATED FAT 0 G | SODIUM 16 MG | CARBS 25 G | FIBER 11 G | SUGARS 12 G
PROTEIN 2 G | CALCIUM 58 MG | IRON 1 MG

radishing raspberry

 IMMUNITY DETOX WEIGHT LOSS ALKALINE UNSWEETENED

This is a brilliant digestive aid and intestinal cleanser. The high water content and fiber in the apples, cucumber, celery, and romaine flushes toxins and cleanses the colon. Celery—a natural laxative, diuretic, and kidney supporter—combines with cucumber to make a complete protein that delivers all of the essential amino acids.

SERVES 2

1 cup (240ml) unfiltered apple juice

2 green apples, skin on, cored and chopped (grated, if using a conventional blender)

1 cup (37g) chopped romaine lettuce

1/2 medium cucumber, chopped

2 small ribs celery, chopped

1 tablespoon freshly squeezed lemon juice

1/2 cup (80g) frozen mango, plus more to taste or as needed

OPTIONAL BOOSTERS

2 tablespoons chopped raw walnuts, soaked (see page 6)

1/4 cup (30g) frozen raw broccoli florets

1 teaspoon wheatgrass powder

Throw all of the ingredients (except the frozen mango) into your blender and blast on high for about 1 minute, until well combined. Add the frozen mango and blast for 10 to 20 seconds more, until smooth and creamy. Add more mango to taste, or as needed to smooth out the texture if you're using a conventional blender.

NUTRITIONAL FACTS (PER SERVING)

CALORIES 194 KCAL | FAT 0 G | SATURATED FAT 0 G | SODIUM 32 MG | CARBS 49 G | FIBER 6 G | SUGARS 38 G
PROTEIN 1 G | CALCIUM 52 MG | IRON 0 MG

appcelerade

INFLAMMATION   IMMUNITY   WEIGHT LOSS   UNSWEETENED   ALKALINE

With a delightful, refreshing flavor, this is the ultimate introductory green smoothie. Loaded with heart-healthy potassium, immune-boosting vitamin C, colon-cleansing fiber, vision-boosting vitamin A, and blood-building iron, this one's got your back. Add the wheatgrass and cayenne for a cleansing kick.

SERVES 2

2 cups (480ml) coconut water or water

2 cups (86g) firmly packed baby spinach

1 medium sliced banana, fresh or frozen

1½ cups (240g) frozen mango

1-inch (2.5cm) piece or 1 tablespoon creamed coconut (see page 234)

OPTIONAL BOOSTERS

1 teaspoon wheatgrass powder

Pinch of finely grated lime zest, plus 1 teaspoon freshly squeezed lime juice

Pinch of cayenne pepper

Throw all of the ingredients into your blender and blast on high for 30 to 60 seconds, until smooth and creamy.

NUTRITIONAL FACTS (PER SERVING)

CALORIES 146 KCAL | FAT 1 G | SATURATED FAT 1 G | SODIUM 45 MG | CARBS 33 G | FIBER 4 G | SUGARS 24 G PROTEIN 2 G | CALCIUM 66 MG | IRON 1 MG

tropical keen and green

DETOX

WEIGHT LOSS

UNSWEETENED

This refreshing vitamin-C buffet (the camu powder booster adds even more) keeps away colds, flu, laryngitis, and sinusitis. Pineapple's bromelain suppresses coughs and loosens mucus, and turmeric reduces inflammation. The bok choy, like the wheatgrass and broccoli boosters, is undetectable and contributes polyphenol antioxidants to combat cancer.

SERVES 2

2 cups (480ml) freshly squeezed orange juice

1 cup (102g) chopped bok choy

2 cups (320g) frozen pineapple

⅛ teaspoon ground turmeric, plus more to taste (optional)

OPTIONAL BOOSTERS

1 teaspoon camu powder

¼ cup (30g) frozen raw broccoli florets

1 teaspoon wheatgrass powder

Throw all of the ingredients into your blender and blast on high for about 1 minute, until smooth and creamy. Tweak turmeric to taste.

NUTRITIONAL FACTS (PER SERVING)

CALORIES 198 KCAL | FAT 0 G | SATURATED FAT 0 G | SODIUM 37 MG | CARBS 47 G | FIBER 3 G | SUGARS 37 G
PROTEIN 3 G | CALCIUM 101 MG | IRON 1 MG

pineapple protector

INFLAMMATION   IMMUNITY   DETOX   WEIGHT LOSS   UNSWEETENED

This sweet treat is brilliant for digestive health. Cranberries help quash yeast growth, cleanse the liver, and stop bacteria from adhering to the urinary tract lining. Antioxidant, anti-inflammatory phytonutrients in cranberries prevent periodontal disease, stomach ulcers, and colon cancer. Bioflavonoids in cherries can alleviate migraines and oxidative stress to slow aging.

SERVES 2

1 ¾ cups (420ml) unfiltered apple juice

½ cup (14g) loosely packed chopped collard greens (about ½ large leaf with stalk removed)

1 cup (120g) frozen cranberries

1 ½ cups (210g) frozen pitted sweet cherries

¼ teaspoon finely grated lemon zest (optional)

OPTIONAL BOOSTERS

Pinch of cayenne pepper

1 tablespoon maqui powder

1 teaspoon coconut oil

Throw all of the ingredients into your blender and blast on high for about 1 minute, until smooth and creamy.

NUTRITIONAL FACTS (PER SERVING)

CALORIES 194 KCAL | FAT 0 G | SATURATED FAT 0 G | SODIUM 11 MG | CARBS 48 G | FIBER 5 G | SUGARS 36 G | PROTEIN 1 G | CALCIUM 38 MG | IRON 0 MG

cleansing cran-cherry

INFLAMMATION   IMMUNITY   DETOX   WEIGHT LOSS   UNSWEETENED

Crammed with phytonutrients, antioxidants, potassium, and fiber, this one's a refreshing, alkalizing detox machine! The ingredients kick up immunity, clear the respiratory tract, cleanse the liver, curb inflammation (great for arthritis), and aid digestive and heart health. The lycopene in red grapefruit also protects skin from UV damage.

SERVES 2

¾ cup (180ml) freshly squeezed orange juice

½ medium red grapefruit, peel and pith removed, seeded, and cut into chunks

1 orange, peeled, seeded, and quartered

1 lime, peeled and halved

1 tangerine or mandarin orange, peeled and seeded

½ medium lemon, peeled and seeded

1 cup (25g) torn-up curly green kale leaves (1 or 2 large leaves with stalk removed)

½ small avocado, pitted and peeled

10 drops alcohol-free liquid stevia, plus more to taste

1 medium frozen sliced banana

1 cup (125g) ice cubes

OPTIONAL BOOSTERS

1 teaspoon camu powder

1 tablespoon chia seeds

¼ cup (30g) frozen raw cauliflower florets

Throw all of the ingredients (except the frozen banana and ice cubes) into your blender and blast on high for 30 to 60 seconds, until smooth. Add the frozen banana and ice cubes and blast for 10 to 20 seconds more, until smooth and creamy. Tweak sweetener to taste.

NUTRITIONAL FACTS (PER SERVING)

CALORIES 240 KCAL | FAT 5 G | SATURATED FAT 0 G | SODIUM 12 MG | CARBS 49 G | FIBER 8 G | SUGARS 29 G
PROTEIN 4 G | CALCIUM 101 MG | IRON 1 MG

citrus saver

 INFLAMMATION

 IMMUNITY

 DETOX

 ALKALINE

 UNSWEETENED

This tangy, refreshing blend (I love adding ginger) is my go-to breakfast. Potent detoxifiers, limes are acidic, but alkaline when metabolized, thanks to their mineral salts—which help liver function and cleanse the colon. This blend is healthy heaven in a glass, but drink it fast, before the stevia develops an aftertaste.

SERVES 2

¾ cup (180ml) coconut water or water

½ cup (90g) young Thai coconut meat or 1 tablespoon creamed coconut

2 cups (86g) firmly packed baby spinach

1 medium avocado, pitted and peeled

½ medium cucumber, chopped

2 teaspoons finely grated lime zest

2 limes, peeled and halved

20 drops alcohol-free liquid stevia, plus more to taste

Pinch of natural salt (optional, to bring out flavors)

1½ cups (190g) ice cubes

OPTIONAL BOOSTERS

1 tablespoon blanched raw almonds, soaked (see page 6)

1 teaspoon minced ginger

1 teaspoon chia seeds

Throw all of the ingredients into your blender and blast on high for 30 to 60 seconds, until smooth and creamy.

NUTRITIONAL FACTS (PER SERVING)

CALORIES 360 KCAL | FAT 30 G | SATURATED FAT 15 G | SODIUM 134 MG | CARBS 26 G | FIBER 14 G | SUGARS 5 G | PROTEIN 5 G | CALCIUM 100 MG | IRON 3 MG

alkaline lime

 INFLAMMATION IMMUNITY DETOX UNSWEETENED ALKALINE

This blend is a satisfying meal replacement—the incredible explosion of flavors tastes like liquid guacamole! Avocados are a complete protein, rich in alkalizing vitamins and minerals, heart-healthy fats, and glutathione, the magical antioxidant that repairs cell and tissue damage, calms inflammation, and regulates metabolism.

SERVES 2

1½ cups (360ml) water

1½ avocados, pitted and peeled

½ medium cucumber, peeled and chopped

¼ cup (7g) firmly packed arugula

¼ cup (7g) finely chopped cilantro

1 tablespoon freshly squeezed lime juice, plus more to taste

1 tablespoon cold-pressed, extra-virgin olive oil

1 teaspoon finely chopped red onion

2 cloves garlic, peeled

¼ teaspoon finely chopped serrano chile, plus more to taste

½ teaspoon natural salt, plus more to taste

1½ cups (190g) ice cubes

OPTIONAL BOOSTERS

1 teaspoon cold-pressed avocado oil

1 teaspoon shelled hemp seeds

½ teaspoon wheatgrass powder

Throw all of the ingredients into your blender and blast on high for 30 to 60 seconds, until smooth and creamy. Tweak flavors to taste (you may like more lime juice, chile, or salt).

NUTRITIONAL FACTS (PER SERVING)

Calories 318 kcal | **Fat** 28 g | **Saturated fat** 4 g | **Sodium** 607 mg | **Carbs** 17 g | **Fiber** 10 g | **Sugars** 2 g **Protein** 3 g | **Calcium** 51 mg | **Iron** 1 mg

avo and cuke cooler

 ENERGIZING   **INFLAMMATION**   **DETOX**   **ALKALINE**   **UNSWEETENED**

This "blendsation" tastes like ice cream and contains a good amount of protein, especially with the boosters. Heart-healthy phytonutrients and fiber from the pears combine with anti-inflammatory ginger to help regulate the digestive system, tone the intestinal tract, and relieve bloating and nausea.

SERVES 2

¾ cup (180ml) unsweetened hemp milk, or other nut, grain, or seed milk (strained if homemade)

1 tablespoon vanilla protein powder

3 ripe pears, skin on, cored and diced

1 cup (27g) loosely packed baby spinach

2 teaspoons freshly squeezed lime juice, plus more to taste

2 teaspoons minced ginger

1 teaspoon shelled hemp seeds

1 chopped pitted date, soaked (see page 6)

½ medium frozen sliced banana

1 cup (125g) ice cubes

OPTIONAL BOOSTERS

1 tablespoon raw almond butter (not peanut butter; it's overpowering)

1 tablespoon chia seeds

½ teaspoon wheatgrass powder

Throw all of the ingredients into your blender and blast on high for 30 to 60 seconds, until smooth and creamy. Tweak lime juice to taste.

NUTRITIONAL FACTS (PER SERVING)

CALORIES 128 KCAL | FAT 1 G | SATURATED FAT 0 G | SODIUM 48 MG | CARBS 26 G | FIBER 3 G | SUGARS 17 G
PROTEIN 3 G | CALCIUM 103 MG | IRON 1 MG

pear-licious perfection

PROTEIN RICH   ENERGIZING   IMMUNITY

This sweet anti cancer crusader contains superior antioxidants and phytonutrients that protect against cellular damage. Pomegranate encourages breast- and prostate-cancer cells to self-destruct, a process heightened by the cancer-crushing power of the quercetin and ellagic acid in the cherries. Boost with cardamom for crazy-good flavor.

SERVES 2

1¾ cups (420ml) unsweetened pomegranate juice

½ cup (14g) chopped collard greens (about ½ large leaf with stalk removed)

2 cups (280g) frozen pitted sweet cherries

½ cup (80g) frozen mango

OPTIONAL BOOSTERS

1 tablespoon açaí powder

⅛ teaspoon ground cardamom

¼ cup (30g) frozen raw broccoli florets

Throw all of the ingredients into your blender and blast on high for 30 to 60 seconds, until smooth and creamy.

NUTRITIONAL FACTS (PER SERVING)

CALORIES 230 KCAL | FAT 1 G | SATURATED FAT 0 G | SODIUM 21 MG | CARBS 57 G | FIBER 3 G | SUGARS 51 G
PROTEIN 2 G | CALCIUM 49 MG | IRON 0 MG

pomegranate power

INFLAMMATION   IMMUNITY   DETOX   UNSWEETENED

This blend is surprisingly sweet and delicious, and the parsley is brilliant for alleviating inflammation, asthma, and airborne allergies. The blend's mineral salts neutralize acids, purify blood, cleanse the skin, detoxify tissues and organs, assist with elimination of heavy metals, flush out the kidneys, and aid urinary tract health.

SERVES 2

³/₄ cup (180ml) coconut water or water

½ English cucumber, chopped

1 bunch flat-leaf parsley, chopped

2 medium lemons, peeled and seeded

2 cups (320g) frozen pineapple

5 drops alcohol-free liquid stevia, plus more to taste

OPTIONAL BOOSTERS

1 teaspoon wheatgrass powder

1 teaspoon minced ginger

¼ cup (30g) frozen raw cauliflower florets

Throw all of the ingredients into your blender and blast on high for about 1 minute, until smooth and creamy. Tweak sweetener to taste.

NUTRITIONAL FACTS (PER SERVING)

CALORIES 118 KCAL | FAT 0 G | SATURATED FAT 0 G | SODIUM 24 MG | CARBS 31 G | FIBER 5 G | SUGARS 18 G
PROTEIN 2 G | CALCIUM 91 MG | IRON 2 MG

allergies be gone!

 INFLAMMATION IMMUNITY DETOX UNSWEETENED WEIGHT LOSS

Mildly flavored radish tops boast more vitamin C, calcium, and protein than their spicy roots! (But if you're wary, romaine or spinach make a great substitute.) The immune-boosting power of the greens and the sweetness of apple and mango make for awesome nutrient and flavor madness!

SERVES 2

2 cups (480ml) coconut water or water

1 apple, skin on, cored and chopped

1 cup (37g) lightly packed radish greens or spinach

1/8 teaspoon ground cinnamon

2 cups (320g) frozen mango

Natural sweetener (optional)

OPTIONAL BOOSTERS

1 tablespoon raw unsalted macadamias, soaked (see page 6)

1 tablespoon flaxseed oil

1 tablespoon chia seeds

Throw all of the ingredients into your blender and blast on high for 30 to 60 seconds, until smooth and creamy.

NUTRITIONAL FACTS (PER SERVING)

CALORIES 146 KCAL | FAT 0 G | SATURATED FAT 0 G | SODIUM 17 MG | CARBS 37 G | FIBER 5 G | SUGARS 31 G
PROTEIN 1 G | CALCIUM 38 MG | IRON 0 MG

apple and mango madness

IMMUNITY

DETOX

WEIGHT LOSS

UNSWEETENED

This spectacular, guilt-free dessert is the ultimate immune system reboot. It's rich in protein (the boosters add even more), alkalizing vitamins and minerals, antioxidants, and healthy fats. Coconut's lauric, capric, and caprylic acids are lethal to lurking microbes. The glutathione in avocado calms inflammation, repairs cell and tissue damage, and regulates metabolism.

SERVES 2

2 cups (480ml) coconut water

1 cup (180g) young Thai coconut meat

1/2 small avocado, pitted and peeled

1 cup (27g) loosely packed baby spinach

1 tablespoon coconut oil

3/4 teaspoon ground cinnamon

1/4 teaspoon ground cardamom

15 drops alcohol-free liquid stevia, plus more to taste

1 cup (125g) ice cubes

OPTIONAL BOOSTERS

1 teaspoon wheatgrass powder

1 tablespoon vanilla protein powder

1 tablespoon raw almond butter

Throw all of the ingredients into your blender and blast on high for 30 to 60 seconds, until smooth and creamy. Tweak sweetener to taste.

NUTRITIONAL FACTS (PER SERVING)

CALORIES 485 KCAL | FAT 42 G | SATURATED FAT 33 G | SODIUM 285 MG | CARBS 27 G | FIBER 13 G | SUGARS 12 G
PROTEIN 5 G | CALCIUM 100 MG | IRON 3 MG

creamy coconut crusader

PROTEIN RICH

INFLAMMATION

IMMUNITY

ALKALINE

UNSWEETENED

This liquid Popsicle is a sneaky green treat for kids. Adults: boost it with mint and lemon zest for a more interesting, heart-healthy sip. Polyphenol antioxidants and potassium in the red grapes regulate blood pressure and cholesterol, and vitamin K (in collards as well) helps with blood clotting. Drink this fast, before the greens assert themselves.

SERVES 2

2 cups (480ml) Concord grape juice

2 cups (340g) frozen red seedless grapes

1/2 cup (14g) chopped collard greens (about 1/2 large leaf with stalk removed)

1/2 small avocado, pitted and peeled

OPTIONAL BOOSTERS

1 teaspoon finely grated lemon zest

2 tablespoons chopped mint

1 tablespoon açaí powder

Throw all of the ingredients into your blender and blast on high for 30 to 60 seconds, until smooth and creamy.

NUTRITIONAL FACTS (PER SERVING)

CALORIES 317 KCAL | FAT 5 G | SATURATED FAT 0 G | SODIUM 30 MG | CARBS 70 G | FIBER 4 G | SUGARS 61 G PROTEIN 2 G | CALCIUM 41 MG | IRON 1 MG

grape guzzler

INFLAMMATION · IMMUNITY · DETOX · UNSWEETENED

Kiwis are great sources of vitamins C and E, potassium, and fiber. They also contain lutein to help lower blood pressure, and are one of the few fruits high in essential fatty acids. Peel your kiwis to avoid a fuzzy mouthfeel. Chia boosts those omega-3s and ginger adds a warm flavor to the blend.

SERVES 2

1 cup (240ml) unsweetened rice milk, hemp milk, or almond milk (strained if homemade)

1/2 cup (120ml) water

3 medium ripe kiwis, peeled and chopped

1 cup (27g) loosely packed baby spinach

1/4 cup (35g) raw unsalted cashews, soaked (see page 6)

1/2 cup (8g) loosely packed mint leaves, plus more to taste

1/2 medium frozen ripe banana

1 cup (125g) ice cubes

OPTIONAL BOOSTERS

1 teaspoon minced ginger

1 tablespoon chia seeds

1/2 teaspoon wheatgrass powder

Throw all of the ingredients into your blender and blast on high for 30 to 60 seconds, until smooth and creamy. Tweak mint to taste.

NUTRITIONAL FACTS (PER SERVING)

CALORIES 223 KCAL | FAT 9 G | SATURATED FAT 1 G | SODIUM 98 MG | CARBS 32 G | FIBER 5 G | SUGARS 17 G PROTEIN 5 G | CALCIUM 301 MG | IRON 2 MG

minty kiwi kreme

CONTAINS NUTS   **UNSWEETENED**

This is a cold-and-flu buster and potent detoxifier, all in one zesty cocktail! The bromelain in pineapple suppresses coughs and loosens mucus, while mint clears respiratory congestion, soothes sore throats, and alleviates nausea. The vitamin C in limes has antibiotic power, anti-inflammatories in kale and pineapple combat arthritis, and ginger boosts immunity, aids digestion, and adds a powerful zing.

SERVES 2

1 cup (240ml) coconut water or water

1 teaspoon finely grated lime zest

3 limes, peeled and quartered

1 cup (25g) torn-up curly green kale leaves (1 or 2 large leaves with stalk removed)

½ cup (18g) firmly packed mint

2 cups (320g) frozen pineapple

5 drops alcohol-free liquid stevia, plus more to taste

OPTIONAL BOOSTERS

1 teaspoon wheatgrass powder

1 teaspoon minced ginger

1 teaspoon coconut oil

Throw all of the ingredients into your blender and blast on high for 30 to 60 seconds, until smooth and creamy.

NUTRITIONAL FACTS (PER SERVING)

CALORIES 118 KCAL | FAT 0 G | SATURATED FAT 0 G | SODIUM 14 MG | CARBS 33 G | FIBER 5 G | SUGARS 17 G
PROTEIN 2 G | CALCIUM 83 MG | IRON 1 MG

green mojito

INFLAMMATION   **IMMUNITY**   **WEIGHT LOSS**   **DETOX**   **UNSWEETENED**

The combination of cashews, bananas, and mint tastes like ice cream, and transforms the otherwise gag-worthy spirulina and chlorella powders into delectable magic. Packed with alkalizing and detoxifying chlorophyll, regenerating protein, and iron—as well as vitamins A, B, and K (even more with the boosters)—this cleansing shake will make you ache for algae.

SERVES 2

1½ cups (360ml) unsweetened almond milk or other nut, grain, or seed milk (strained if homemade)

1 teaspoon wheatgrass powder

½ teaspoon spirulina powder

½ teaspoon chlorella powder

1 cup (43g) firmly packed baby spinach

¾ cup (105g) raw unsalted cashews, soaked (see page 6)

¼ cup (9g) firmly packed mint

½ teaspoon natural vanilla extract

¼ teaspoon mint extract, plus more to taste

1 tablespoon coconut nectar or other liquid sweetener

2 large frozen sliced bananas

1 cup (125g) ice cubes

OPTIONAL BOOSTERS

1 tablespoon vanilla protein powder or chocolate protein powder

1 tablespoon avocado oil

1 tablespoon shelled hemp seeds

Throw all of the ingredients into your blender and blast on high for 30 to 60 seconds, until smooth and creamy.

NUTRITIONAL FACTS (PER SERVING)

CALORIES 230 KCAL | FAT 12 G | SATURATED FAT 10 G | SODIUM 161 MG | CARBS 31 G | FIBER 3 G | SUGARS 25 G | PROTEIN 2 G | CALCIUM 40 MG | IRON 2 MG

minty green gluttony

CONTAINS NUTS   ENERGIZING   DETOX

This bold cleansing combo blends up a sweet and musky flavor. Its glorious green ingredients are hydrating, detoxifying, and loaded with fiber and antioxidants to aid digestion, enhance bowel function, break down toxins, and boost immunity. For a real mover, ramp up the flavor and anti-inflammatory power with ginger and cayenne.

SERVES 2

$\frac{1}{2}$ cup (120ml) coconut water or water

1 green apple, skin on, cored and chopped

1 cup (170g) seedless green grapes

1 small rib celery, chopped

1 cup (25g) torn-up curly green kale leaves (1 or 2 large leaves with stalk removed)

$\frac{1}{2}$ small fennel bulb, cored, trimmed of stalks, and chopped

1 medium lemon, peeled and seeded

1$\frac{1}{2}$ cups (240g) frozen pineapple

OPTIONAL BOOSTERS

1 teaspoon wheatgrass powder

1 teaspoon minced ginger

Pinch of cayenne pepper

Throw all of the ingredients (except the frozen pineapple) into your blender and blast on high for 30 to 60 seconds, until well combined. Add the frozen pineapple and blast for 10 to 20 seconds more, until smooth and chilled.

NUTRITIONAL FACTS (PER SERVING)

CALORIES 195 KCAL | FAT 0 G | SATURATED FAT 0 G | SODIUM 44 MG | CARBS 51 G | FIBER 7 G | SUGARS 35 G
PROTEIN 2 G | CALCIUM 81 MG | IRON 1 MG

green grappler

INFLAMMATION

IMMUNITY

WEIGHT LOSS

UNSWEETENED

DETOX

This blends a light, fresh flavor (don't miss the mint) with the warming flavor of ginger. The chard and berries offer astonishing antioxidants (boost with açaí and chia for even more) and protect the brain from oxidative stress, providing anti-inflammatory and detox support. Drink immediately, before the chard gets bossy.

SERVES 2

2 cups (480ml) water

1 cup (31g) firmly packed chard leaves

1 medium frozen sliced banana

½ teaspoon minced ginger, plus more to taste

⅛ teaspoon finely grated lemon zest, plus more to taste

1 cup (160g) frozen blackberries

1 cup (160g) frozen blueberries

Natural sweetener (optional)

OPTIONAL BOOSTERS

1 tablespoon açaí powder

2 tablespoons chopped mint

1 teaspoon chia seeds

Throw all of the ingredients into your blender and blast on high for 30 to 60 seconds, until smooth and creamy. Tweak flavors to taste (you may like a bit more ginger, zest, or sweetener).

NUTRITIONAL FACTS (PER SERVING)

CALORIES 135 KCAL | FAT 0 G | SATURATED FAT 0 G | SODIUM 44 MG | CARBS 33 G | FIBER 7 G | SUGARS 19 G
PROTEIN 2 G | CALCIUM 46 MG | IRON 1 MG

chard black and blue

INFLAMMATION DETOX WEIGHT LOSS UNSWEETENED

This detox blend is intensely hydrating and alkalizing. The pectin and mineral salts in the apples combine with the oxalic acid in the spinach for a powerful laxative effect to alleviate constipation and cleanse the colon. Cayenne gets things moving, too—but use a light hand or it'll set your mouth on fire!

SERVES 2

½ cup (120ml) coconut water or water

2 green apples, skin on, cored and roughly chopped (grated, if using a conventional blender)

1 cup (27g) loosely packed baby spinach

1 medium lemon, peeled, seeded, and quartered

½ medium cucumber, chopped

1 teaspoon minced ginger

10 drops alcohol-free liquid stevia, plus more to taste

1 cup (125g) ice cubes

OPTIONAL BOOSTERS

Pinch of cayenne pepper

½ teaspoon wheatgrass powder

1 tablespoon chia seeds

Throw all of the ingredients (except the ice cubes) into your blender and blast on high for about 1 minute, until smooth. Add the ice and blast for a few seconds more, until smooth and chilled.

NUTRITIONAL FACTS (PER SERVING)

CALORIES 115 KCAL | FAT 0 G | SATURATED FAT 0 G | SODIUM 19 MG | CARBS 30 G | FIBER 5 G | SUGARS 20 G PROTEIN 1 G | CALCIUM 45 MG | IRON 0 MG

apple alkalaid

INFLAMMATION   DETOX   WEIGHT LOSS   ALKALINE   UNSWEETENED

The sharp flavor of dandelion greens in this glorious tropical concoction fools even the most skeptical cocktail aficionados into thinking there's a nip of alcohol in the mix. Sweeten to your preference and based on the ripeness of your pineapple. Spike it with all three boosters for added cleansing benefits and rich flavor.

SERVES 2

1½ cups (360ml) canned coconut milk (shake, then pour)

½ cup (120ml) coconut water

2 teaspoons freshly squeezed lime juice

3 cups (480g) frozen pineapple

½ cup (7g) loosely packed dandelion greens (optional)

1 tablespoon pure maple syrup, plus more to taste (optional)

OPTIONAL BOOSTERS

1 tablespoon coconut oil

1 teaspoon wheatgrass powder

1 tablespoon vanilla protein powder

Throw all of the ingredients into your blender and blast on high for 30 to 60 seconds, until smooth and creamy. Add more maple syrup to taste.

NUTRITIONAL FACTS (PER SERVING)

CALORIES 493 KCAL | FAT 36 G | SATURATED FAT 32 G | SODIUM 89 MG | CARBS 45 G | FIBER 4 G | SUGARS 31 G PROTEIN 5 G | CALCIUM 88 MG | IRON 6 MG

piña colada

ENERGIZING   **INFLAMMATION**

Peppery arugula creates a sweet and savory harmony with pear and apple; add the celery, walnuts, and flaxseed oil for a dimensional salad sensation. Antioxidants in pears neutralize free radicals and cancer-causing toxins, while detoxifying enzymes in arugula cast out pesticides, herbicides, and heavy metals.

SERVES 2

1 cup (240ml) unfiltered apple juice

3 ripe pears, skin on, cored and diced

½ cup (14g) firmly packed arugula

1 cup (125g) ice cubes

OPTIONAL BOOSTERS

1 small rib celery, diced

2 tablespoons raw walnuts, soaked (see page 6)

1 tablespoon flaxseed oil

Throw all of the ingredients into your blender and blast on high for 30 to 60 seconds, until smooth and creamy.

NUTRITIONAL FACTS (PER SERVING)

CALORIES 58 KCAL | FAT 0 G | SATURATED FAT 0 G | SODIUM 9 MG | CARBS 14 G | FIBER 0 G | SUGARS 12 G
PROTEIN 0 G | CALCIUM 22 MG | IRON 0 MG

pear and arugula salad

ENERGIZING   **DETOX**   **WEIGHT LOSS**   **UNSWEETENED**

This vegetable-packed blend is surprisingly delicious (definitely add the mint!). The betaine in beets flushes the liver, purifies the blood, and enhances circulation; carrots boost the liver's antioxidant capacity; and lemons improve liver function. Chard provides syringic acid, a flavonoid that prevents liver degeneration, and mango and ginger have liver-protecting properties, too.

SERVES 2

1½ cups (360ml) unfiltered apple juice

1 medium raw beet, chopped (steamed or baked, if using a conventional blender)

1 medium carrot, chopped (steamed or grated, if using a conventional blender)

2 medium lemons, peeled and seeded

1 cup (31g) loosely packed chard leaves

1 teaspoon minced ginger (optional)

1 cup (160g) frozen mango

OPTIONAL BOOSTERS

¼ cup (9g) firmly packed mint

¼ cup (30g) frozen raw broccoli florets

⅛ teaspoon ground turmeric

Throw all of the ingredients (except the frozen mango) into your blender and blast on high for about 1 minute, until well combined. Add the frozen mango and blast for 10 to 20 seconds more, until smooth and creamy.

NUTRITIONAL FACTS (PER SERVING)

CALORIES 177 KCAL | FAT 0 G | SATURATED FAT 0 G | SODIUM 82 MG | CARBS 44 G | FIBER 4 G | SUGARS 33 G
PROTEIN 2 G | CALCIUM 60 MG | IRON 1 MG

liver lover

INFLAMMATION   IMMUNITY   DETOX   WEIGHT LOSS   UNSWEETENED

This stunner bursts with complex flavors that will dance on the tip of your tongue and tease your throat long after they've massaged your belly. Boost the pineapple's cleansing and anti-inflammatory power with a hit of wheatgrass, turmeric, and olive oil. It's not to be missed.

SERVES 2

1½ cups (360ml) coconut water or water

1 cup (43g) firmly packed baby spinach

2 teaspoons finely chopped red onion, plus more to taste

2 tablespoons chopped cucumber

½ cup (14g) finely chopped cilantro

1 teaspoon finely chopped jalapeño chile, plus more to taste

2 tablespoons freshly squeezed lime juice, plus more to taste

¼ teaspoon finely grated lime zest

¼ teaspoon natural salt

3 cups (480g) frozen pineapple

Natural sweetener (optional)

OPTIONAL BOOSTERS

1 teaspoon cold-pressed extra-virgin olive oil

1 teaspoon wheatgrass powder

⅛ teaspoon ground turmeric

Throw all of the ingredients into your blender and blast on high for about 1 minute, until smooth and creamy. Tweak flavors to taste (you may want more onion, jalapeño, lime juice, salt, or sweetener, depending on the ripeness of your pineapple).

NUTRITIONAL FACTS (PER SERVING)

CALORIES 133 KCAL | FAT 0 G | SATURATED FAT 0 G | SODIUM 321 MG | CARBS 34 G | FIBER 4 G | SUGARS 24 G
PROTEIN 2 G | CALCIUM 67 MG | IRON 1 MG

pineapple salsa

INFLAMMATION

IMMUNITY

DETOX

WEIGHT LOSS

This sip is sensational for your skin. Tangerines and peaches are loaded with vitamin C, which is crucial for the synthesis of collagen to help heal injured tissues and hold together tendons, ligaments, bones, and blood vessels. Rosemary stimulates cell regeneration and adds a magical flavor.

SERVES 2

1½ cups (360ml) unsweetened tangerine juice

3 tangerines or mandarin oranges, peeled and seeded

¾ teaspoon finely chopped rosemary

1 teaspoon coconut nectar or pure maple syrup, plus more to taste

2 cups (320g) frozen peaches

OPTIONAL BOOSTERS

¼ cup (30g) frozen raw cauliflower florets

1 teaspoon camu powder

1 teaspoon hemp oil

Throw all of the ingredients into your blender and blast on high for 30 to 60 seconds, until smooth and creamy. Tweak sweetener to taste.

NUTRITIONAL FACTS (PER SERVING)

CALORIES 151 KCAL | FAT 0 G | SATURATED FAT 0 G | SODIUM 2 MG | CARBS 36 G | FIBER 2 G | SUGARS 33 G PROTEIN 2 G | CALCIUM 48 MG | IRON 0 MG

tangerine twist

ENERGIZING   IMMUNITY   DETOX   WEIGHT LOSS

I think of this powerful immunity blend as "field to shield." With the antioxidant weight of these ingredients, nothing's gettin' the better of you (especially if you boost with açaí, maqui, and chia seeds)! The trio of orange zest, cinnamon, and ginger warms up the party, making this "berry" special.

SERVES 2

1¼ cups (300ml) coconut water or water, plus more as needed

2 cups (320g) mixed fresh or frozen berries (½ cup /80g each of blueberries, blackberries, raspberries, and strawberries)

½ cup (85g) red seedless grapes

1 ripe pear, skin on, cored and diced

½ teaspoon minced ginger

¼ teaspoon ground cinnamon

½ teaspoon finely grated orange zest

1 chopped pitted date, soaked (see page 6), plus more to taste

1 cup (125g) ice cubes

OPTIONAL BOOSTERS

2 tablespoons açaí powder

2 teaspoons maqui powder

1 tablespoon chia seeds

Throw all of the ingredients into your blender and blast on high for 30 to 60 seconds, until smooth and creamy. Add more coconut water as needed to blend. Tweak the sweetness to taste.

NUTRITIONAL FACTS (PER SERVING)

CALORIES 256 KCAL | FAT 1 G | SATURATED FAT 0 G | SODIUM 12 MG | CARBS 66 G | FIBER 9 G | SUGARS 48 G PROTEIN 2 G | CALCIUM 43 MG | IRON 1 MG

antioxidant avenger

INFLAMMATION   IMMUNITY   DETOX

With a complex, mind-blowing flavor that explodes like a firecracker (don't omit the cayenne), this is a heart-healthy delight. Pomegranate lowers blood pressure, keeps arteries supple, decreases inflammation in blood vessels, and helps manage cholesterol. Its phenolic antioxidants (also in strawberries) combat oxidative stress, making this an antiaging tonic.

SERVES 2

1½ cups (360ml) unsweetened pomegranate juice

1 orange, peeled, seeded, and quartered

¼ cup (35g) chopped red bell pepper

⅛ cup (3g) loosely packed arugula

½ small avocado, pitted and peeled

1 cup (160g) frozen strawberries

1 cup (125g) ice cubes

OPTIONAL BOOSTERS

1 tablespoon pomegranate powder

½ cup (15g) loosely packed chard leaves

Pinch of cayenne pepper

Throw all of the ingredients into your blender and blast on high for about 1 minute, until smooth and creamy.

NUTRITIONAL FACTS (PER SERVING)

CALORIES 232 KCAL | FAT 6 G | SATURATED FAT 0 G | SODIUM 23 MG | CARBS 45 G | FIBER 6 G | SUGARS 37 G
PROTEIN 2 G | CALCIUM 79 MG | IRON 0 MG

pomegranate slam it!

 INFLAMMATION IMMUNITY DETOX   ALKALINE UNSWEETENED

These flavors explode up front, expand in the mouth, and party in your throat till the next sip hits your lips. This potent alkalizer, immune booster, and anti-inflammatory aid is also awesome for weight loss. And guys: the lutein in the avocado plus the lycopene in the tomato equals prostate-cancer prevention.

SERVES 2

2 tomatoes, chopped

1/2 red bell pepper, seeded and chopped

1/2 medium cucumber, chopped

1/2 small avocado, pitted and peeled

1 tablespoon finely chopped red onion, plus more to taste

2 tablespoons finely chopped cilantro

2 tablespoons freshly squeezed lime juice, plus more to taste

3/4 teaspoon natural salt, plus more to taste

1/8 teaspoon freshly ground black pepper

Pinch of red pepper flakes

1 cup (125g) ice cubes

OPTIONAL BOOSTERS

1/2 teaspoon finely chopped jalapeño chile

1 tablespoon cold-pressed extra-virgin olive oil

1/4 teaspoon finely grated lime zest

Throw the tomatoes into your blender, then pile on the rest of the ingredients. Blast on high for 30 to 60 seconds, until well combined. Tweak flavors to taste (you may want more onion, lime juice, or salt).

NUTRITIONAL FACTS (PER SERVING)

CALORIES 104 KCAL | FAT 5 G | SATURATED FAT 0 G | SODIUM 887 MG | CARBS 13 G | FIBER 5 G | SUGARS 6 G
PROTEIN 2 G | CALCIUM 36 MG | IRON 0 MG

spicy gazpacho grab

INFLAMMATION   DETOX   WEIGHT LOSS   ALKALINE   UNSWEETENED

Rich in the antioxidant betaine, beets flush the liver, stimulate the lymphatic system, and oxygenate the blood. This blend's flavor is sweet and spicy—far from earthy—thanks to strawberries, apple, lemon, cinnamon, and cayenne. The ingredients power this potent antioxidant, anti-inflammatory, alkalizing, detoxifying, weight-loss machine.

SERVES 2

1¼ cups (300ml) coconut water or water (plus more as needed)

1 medium red beet (cooked, if using a conventional blender), peeled and chopped

1 apple, skin on, cored and chopped

½ small avocado, pitted and peeled

½ lemon, peeled and seeded

⅛ teaspoon ground cinnamon, plus more to taste

Pinch of cayenne pepper

2 cups (320g) frozen strawberries

5 drops alcohol-free liquid stevia, plus more to taste (optional)

OPTIONAL BOOSTERS

1 tablespoon açaí powder

1 teaspoon flaxseed oil

1 teaspoon chia seeds

Throw all of the ingredients into your blender and blast on high for about 1 minute, until smooth and creamy.

NUTRITIONAL FACTS (PER SERVING)

Calories 171 kcal | Fat 5 g | Saturated fat 0 g | Sodium 30 mg | Carbs 31 g | Fiber 8 g | Sugars 19 g Protein 2 g | Calcium 49 mg | Iron 1 mg

berry-beet bliss

INFLAMMATION   IMMUNITY   DETOX   WEIGHT LOSS   UNSWEETENED

This bizarre-sounding combo of vitamin C champions (orange, strawberries, sweet potato, and red bell pepper) creates a delicious immunity blend that's also a great way to get kids to drink their vegetables. For added anti-inflammatory power, throw in the goji berries, ground flaxseeds, and turmeric.

SERVES 2

1 cup (240ml) freshly squeezed orange juice

1 orange, peeled, seeded, and quartered

½ cup (70g) mashed cooked orange sweet potato

½ cup (60g) frozen raw cauliflower florets

¼ cup (35g) diced red bell pepper

¼ cup (30g) blanched raw almonds, soaked (see page 6)

1½ teaspoons finely grated orange zest, plus more to taste

½ teaspoon natural vanilla extract

1½ teaspoons pure maple syrup, plus more to taste

1 cup (160g) frozen strawberries

2 cups (250g) ice cubes

OPTIONAL BOOSTERS

1 tablespoon goji powder

1 teaspoon ground flaxseeds

Pinch of ground turmeric

Throw all of the ingredients into your blender and blast on high for 30 to 60 seconds, until smooth and creamy.

NUTRITIONAL FACTS (PER SERVING)

CALORIES 271 KCAL | **FAT** 8 G | **SATURATED FAT** 0 G | **SODIUM** 36 MG | **CARBS** 46 G | **FIBER** 8 G | **SUGARS** 29 G
PROTEIN 6 G | **CALCIUM** 132 MG | **IRON** 1 MG

creamy orange c

PROTEIN RICH

CONTAINS NUTS

INFLAMMATION

IMMUNITY

This crisp refresher burns fat while it cools, calms, and detoxifies. Steep the tea lightly, and add all boosters for full flavor. Green tea's rich polyphenol antioxidants and alkaloids have anti-inflammatory, chemotherapeutic powers that combat ovarian, breast, and prostate cancer cells. Enzymes in pineapple and grapes also work for cancer prevention.

SERVES 2

1 green tea bag

¾ cup (180ml) boiling water

½ cup (120ml) unfiltered apple juice

1 cup (170g) green seedless grapes

¼ cup (9g) firmly packed mint

2 cups (320g) frozen pineapple

OPTIONAL BOOSTERS

1 teaspoon wheatgrass powder

1 teaspoon minced ginger

Pinch of cayenne pepper

In a small bowl, steep the tea bag in the boiling water for 30 seconds. Remove and discard the bag, allow the tea to cool, and refrigerate until fully chilled. Throw the chilled tea, apple juice, grapes, mint, and pineapple into your blender and blast on high for 30 to 60 seconds, until smooth and creamy.

NUTRITIONAL FACTS (PER SERVING)

CALORIES 169 KCAL | FAT 0 G | SATURATED FAT 0 G | SODIUM 10 MG | CARBS 43 G | FIBER 3 G | SUGARS 34 G
PROTEIN 1 G | CALCIUM 45 MG | IRON 1 MG

green tea-ni

INFLAMMATION   DETOX   WEIGHT LOSS   UNSWEETENED

A surprisingly stunning combination, grapefruit and fennel are both rich in vitamin C, phytonutrients, antioxidants, and potassium. The blend serves up anti-inflammatory, anticancer, weight-loss, and detox power that helps boost immunity, scavenge harmful free radicals, cleanse the colon, regulate heart rate and blood pressure, aid digestion, and alleviate stomach ailments.

SERVES 2

$1/2$ cup (120ml) water

$1/2$ small fennel bulb, cored, trimmed of stalks, and chopped

1 medium red grapefruit, peel and pith removed, seeded, and cut into chunks

1 green apple, skin on, cored and chopped

$1/4$ medium avocado, pitted and peeled

$1 1/2$ tablespoons freshly squeezed lemon juice

15 drops alcohol-free liquid stevia, plus more to taste

$1 1/2$ cups (190g) ice cubes

OPTIONAL BOOSTERS

1 cup (27g) loosely packed baby spinach

1 teaspoon flaxseed oil

1 teaspoon pomegranate powder

Throw all of the ingredients (except the ice cubes) into your blender and blast on high for 30 to 60 seconds, until smooth and creamy. Add the ice and blend for a few seconds more, until smooth and chilled.

NUTRITIONAL FACTS (PER SERVING)

CALORIES 154 KCAL | FAT 4 G | SATURATED FAT 0 G | SODIUM 30 MG | CARBS 31 G | FIBER 7 G | SUGARS 18 G
PROTEIN 2 G | CALCIUM 60 MG | IRON 0 MG

grapefruit-fennel fix

IMMUNITY

DETOX

WEIGHT LOSS

ALKALINE

UNSWEETENED

This is a sweet, smooth mover! The anthraquinone in aloe vera is a laxative and the high-fiber, anti-inflammatory fruits aid digestion and weight loss and flush toxins. Add the cayenne to fire up your lymph and speed things along. Vitamin A (in peaches) and the flavonoids (in all three fruits) are great for skin, reducing swelling and improving elasticity.

SERVES 2

1½ cups (360ml) coconut water

½ cup (120ml) freshly squeezed orange juice

¼ cup (60ml) unsweetened aloe vera juice

1 cup (160g) frozen strawberries

1 cup (160g) frozen peaches

½ cup (80g) frozen pineapple

2 chopped pitted dates, soaked (see page 6)

Pinch of cayenne pepper (optional)

OPTIONAL BOOSTERS

¼ cup (30g) frozen raw broccoli florets

1 tablespoon ground flaxseeds

1 tablespoon blanched raw almonds, soaked (see page 6)

Throw all of the ingredients into your blender and blast on high for 30 to 60 seconds, until smooth and creamy.

NUTRITIONAL FACTS (PER SERVING)

Calories 246 kcal | Fat 1 g | Saturated fat 1 g | Sodium 191 mg | Carbs 60 g | Fiber 8 g | Sugars 49 g
Protein 4 g | Calcium 98 mg | Iron 1 mg

aloe accelerator

IMMUNITY BOOST **DETOX** **WEIGHT LOSS**

This powerhouse of alkalizing minerals (be fearless with the mineral-rich salt) and anti-inflammatory agents (add turmeric for even more) is the ultimate reboot. The chlorophyll in kale oxygenates the blood, and the lauric and caprylic acids in coconut make this blend an antiviral and antibacterial machine. It's also just delicious!

SERVES 2

1/2 cup (120ml) water

1 cup (25g) torn-up curly green kale leaves (1 or 2 large leaves with stalk removed)

1 medium tomato, chopped

1/2 medium cucumber, chopped

1 small avocado, pitted and peeled

1 lime, peeled and halved

1 tablespoon creamed coconut

1 clove garlic, peeled

1 teaspoon natural salt

1 1/2 cups (190g) ice cubes

OPTIONAL BOOSTERS

1 tablespoon cold-pressed extra-virgin olive oil

1/2 cup (50g) frozen raw broccoli florets

Pinch of ground turmeric

Throw all of the ingredients into your blender and blast on high for 30 to 60 seconds, until smooth and creamy.

NUTRITIONAL FACTS (PER SERVING)

CALORIES 163 KCAL | FAT 11 G | SATURATED FAT 2 G | SODIUM 1185 MG | CARBS 16 G | FIBER 7 G | SUGARS 3 G
PROTEIN 3 G | CALCIUM 60 MG | IRON 1 MG

salty alkalaid

INFLAMMATION   **DETOX**   **WEIGHT LOSS**   **ALKALINE**   **UNSWEETENED**

Here, sweet meets heat. Chile fires up your lymphatic system, lime cleanses the liver, and enzymes in mango kick-start protein digestion. Antibiotic flavonoids and polyphenolic antioxidants in mango don't just boost immunity, they also crush cancer cells. And the vitamin E works wonders for skin health and sex drive. Spice things up!

SERVES 2

2 cups (480ml) coconut water

½ teaspoon finely grated lime zest

1 lime, peeled and halved

½ teaspoon finely chopped serrano chile, plus more to taste

2 cups (320g) frozen mango

OPTIONAL BOOSTERS

1 tablespoon coconut oil

1 tablespoon chia seeds

1 teaspoon camu powder

Throw all of the ingredients into your blender and blast on high for 30 to 60 seconds, until smooth and creamy. Tweak chile to taste.

NUTRITIONAL FACTS (PER SERVING)

CALORIES 152 KCAL | FAT 1 G | SATURATED FAT 0 G | SODIUM 254 MG | CARBS 36 G | FIBER 6 G | SUGARS 28 G
PROTEIN 3 G | CALCIUM 86 MG | IRON 1 MG

spicy mango magic

IMMUNITY   DETOX   WEIGHT LOSS   UNSWEETENED

This fresh and fabulous flusher has a multidimensional tang (add stevia to taste) that keeps the liver detoxing at full speed. Cranberry juice, cranberries, and red grapes are rich in antioxidants and quinine, which help cleanse the kidneys of urea, uric acid, and other toxins. Add the boosters for more cleansing power.

SERVES 2

1 cup (240ml) unfiltered apple juice

½ cup (120ml) unsweetened cranberry juice

1 cup (160g) red seedless grapes

¼ cup (35g) diced red bell pepper

1 cup (120g) frozen cranberries

1 cup (140g) frozen pitted sweet cherries

OPTIONAL BOOSTERS

¼ cup (30g) frozen raw cauliflower florets

1 cup (27g) loosely packed baby spinach

1 teaspoon maqui powder

Throw all of the ingredients into your blender and blast on high for 30 to 60 seconds, until smooth and creamy.

NUTRITIONAL FACTS (PER SERVING)

CALORIES 218 KCAL | FAT 0 G | SATURATED FAT 0 G | SODIUM 9 MG | CARBS 55 G | FIBER 5 G | SUGARS 44 G
PROTEIN 2 G | CALCIUM 38 MG | IRON 1 MG

kidney cleanser

INFLAMMATION   IMMUNITY   DETOX   WEIGHT LOSS   UNSWEETENED

This combo delivers omega-3 fatty acids, the antioxidants lutein and zeaxanthin, and vitamins A, C, and E to promote ocular health and stave off age-related vision problems like macular degeneration and cataracts. The broccoli, cauliflower, and goji boosters add vision vigor but leave the delicious, warming flavor untouched.

SERVES 2

1¼ cups (300ml) unsweetened almond milk (strained if homemade)

1 orange, peeled, seeded, and quartered

2 medium carrots, chopped (steamed or grated, if using a conventional blender)

1 teaspoon minced ginger

½ teaspoon ground cinnamon

1 medium frozen sliced banana

1 cup (125g) ice cubes

OPTIONAL BOOSTERS

1 tablespoon goji powder

¼ cup (30g) frozen raw broccoli florets

¼ cup (30g) frozen raw cauliflower florets

Put the almond milk and orange quarters into your blender, add the carrots, and blast on high for about 1 minute, until pureed. Add the remaining ingredients and blend on high for 10 to 20 seconds more, until smooth and creamy.

NUTRITIONAL FACTS (PER SERVING)

CALORIES 160 KCAL | FAT 1 G | SATURATED FAT 0 G | SODIUM 139 MG | CARBS 35 G | FIBER 6 G | SUGARS 23 G PROTEIN 2 G | CALCIUM 350 MG | IRON 0 MG

vivid vision

CONTAINS NUTS   ENERGIZING   IMMUNITY   UNSWEETENED

This is a bold, alkalizing, and cleansing pick-me-up. Add more Worcestershire (I use a gluten-free, vegan version; see page 241), Tabasco, horseradish, and lemon juice for an even bloodier experience. Try salting the rim of your glass and serving with a celery stick—you won't even miss the vodka.

SERVES 2

3 medium tomatoes, chopped

2 tablespoons tomato paste

1/2 cup (66g) diced celery (about 2 ribs)

1/2 medium avocado, pitted and peeled

1 tablespoon minced fresh horseradish (not horseradish sauce), plus more to taste

2 1/2 teaspoons Worcestershire sauce, plus more to taste

10 dashes Tabasco sauce, plus more to taste

2 1/2 tablespoons freshly squeezed lemon juice, plus more to taste

1 teaspoon finely chopped red onion

1 clove garlic, peeled

1 teaspoon natural salt

Pinch of freshly ground black pepper, plus more to taste

2 cups (250g) ice cubes

OPTIONAL BOOSTERS

2 teaspoons cold-pressed extra-virgin olive oil

1 teaspoon chia seeds

1 teaspoon goji powder

Throw all of the ingredients into your blender and blast on high for about 1 minute, until smooth and creamy. Tweak flavors to taste (you may want more horseradish, Worcestershire, Tabasco, lemon juice, or pepper).

NUTRITIONAL FACTS (PER SERVING)

CALORIES 148 KCAL | FAT 8 G | SATURATED FAT 1 G | SODIUM 1460 MG | CARBS 19 G | FIBER 7 G | SUGARS 9 G PROTEIN 3 G | CALCIUM 64 MG | IRON 1 MG

bloody mary might be

INFLAMMATION   DETOX   WEIGHT LOSS   ALKALINE   UNSWEETENED

A powerful immunity aid, carrots boost the production and performance of white blood cells to keep the respiratory system infection resistant. The phytonutrients in the costarring orange juice and flesh are great for the skin, stimulating collagen formation, alleviating psoriasis and eczema, and protecting against oxidative damage. Add the mint and turmeric boosters to spike flavor fever.

SERVES 2

1 cup (240ml) fresh carrot juice

1 cup (240ml) freshly squeezed orange juice

1 medium orange, peeled, seeded, and quartered

1 cup (160g) frozen mango

1 cup (160g) frozen peaches

OPTIONAL BOOSTERS

¼ cup (9g) firmly packed mint

1 teaspoon camu powder

⅛ teaspoon ground turmeric

Throw all of the ingredients into your blender and blast on high for 30 to 60 seconds, until smooth and creamy.

NUTRITIONAL FACTS (PER SERVING)

CALORIES 212 KCAL | FAT 1 G | SATURATED FAT 0 G | SODIUM 79 MG | CARBS 51 G | FIBER 5 G | SUGARS 38 G PROTEIN 3 G | CALCIUM 81 MG | IRON 1 MG

orange ecstasy

INFLAMMATION   **IMMUNITY**   **DETOX**   **UNSWEETENED**

There's great stuff for your brain here—so go nuts! Vitamins C and K and carotenoids in broccoli and cauliflower enhance brain function. Vitamin E in walnuts, almonds, flaxseed, and chia reduce cognitive decline. Blueberries protect the brain from oxidative stress and may reduce age-related degeneration due to Alzheimer's and dementia.

SERVES 2

2 cups (480ml) unsweetened almond milk or other nut, grain, or seed milk (strained if homemade)

1 medium banana

¼ cup (30g) frozen raw cauliflower florets

¼ cup (25g) frozen raw broccoli florets

1 tablespoon raw walnuts, soaked (see page 6)

1 tablespoon raw almond butter

1 tablespoon pure maple syrup, plus more to taste

1½ cups (240g) frozen blueberries

OPTIONAL BOOSTERS

1 tablespoon açaí powder

1 tablespoon chia seeds

1 tablespoon ground flaxseeds

Throw all of the ingredients into your blender and blast on high for about 1 minute, until smooth and creamy. Tweak sweetener to taste.

NUTRITIONAL FACTS (PER SERVING)

CALORIES 289 KCAL | FAT 9 G | SATURATED FAT 0 G | SODIUM 164 MG | CARBS 49 G | FIBER 7 G | SUGARS 33 G
PROTEIN 5 G | CALCIUM 513 MG | IRON 1 MG

brain blast

PROTEIN RICH   CONTAINS NUTS   ENERGIZING

This delicious skin rejuvenator is comforting (with the warming spices) and has an exquisite musky flavor. Rich in vitamins (A, C, and E), fiber, folate, and the protein-digesting enzymes papain and chymopapain, papayas aid digestion, relieve inflammatory conditions like asthma and arthritis, and support heart and colon health. This is the ultimate detox smoothie.

SERVES 2

1½ cups (360ml) unsweetened almond milk (strained if homemade)

2 cups (320g) roughly chopped papaya

2 teaspoons freshly squeezed lemon juice

2 teaspoons minced ginger, plus more to taste

⅛ teaspoon ground cinnamon, plus more to taste

⅛ teaspoon finely grated lemon zest, plus more to taste

5 drops alcohol-free liquid stevia, plus more to taste

¾ cup (120g) frozen mango

1 cup (125g) ice cubes

OPTIONAL BOOSTERS

1 tablespoon flaxseed oil

1 tablespoon shelled hemp seeds

1 tablespoon goji powder

Throw all of the ingredients into your blender and blast on high for about 1 minute, until smooth and creamy. Tweak flavors to taste (you may want more ginger, cinnamon, lemon zest, or sweetener).

NUTRITIONAL FACTS (PER SERVING)

CALORIES 152 KCAL | FAT 2 G | SATURATED FAT 0 G | SODIUM 129 MG | CARBS 33 G | FIBER 4 G | SUGARS 26 G
PROTEIN 2 G | CALCIUM 381 MG | IRON 1 MG

papaya pleasure

CONTAINS NUTS   INFLAMMATION   IMMUNITY   DETOX

Turmeric milk is used to relieve cold and flu symptoms, settle the stomach, relax the body, and aid sleep. This spiced pistachio spin inspired by a classic Indian combo packs loads of protein, fiber, calcium, iron, and vitamin E. Add all three boosters for added nutrition. This blend is my favorite bedtime comfort food.

SERVES 2

2 cups (480ml) unsweetened almond milk (strained if homemade)

½ cup (66g) unsalted shelled pistachios

¼ cup (43g) chopped pitted dates, soaked (see page 6)

1 teaspoon ground cinnamon

¼ teaspoon ground turmeric

¼ teaspoon minced ginger

1 medium frozen sliced banana

1 cup (125g) ice cubes

OPTIONAL BOOSTERS

¼ cup (30g) frozen raw cauliflower florets

1 cup (27g) loosely packed baby spinach

1 teaspoon avocado oil

Throw all of the ingredients (except the frozen banana and ice cubes) into your blender and blast on high for 30 to 60 seconds, until smooth and creamy. Add the frozen banana and ice cubes and blast for about 10 seconds more, until smooth and chilled.

NUTRITIONAL FACTS (PER SERVING)

CALORIES 361 KCAL | FAT 17 G | SATURATED FAT 1 G | SODIUM 155 MG | CARBS 47 G | FIBER 8 G | SUGARS 31 G PROTEIN 8 G | CALCIUM 518 MG | IRON 2 MG

sleep spell

PROTEIN RICH   CONTAINS NUTS

A spicy salad in a glass, this one will get you rolling! Don't be afraid of the onion and liquid aminos—they add a dramatic, magical middle note. With alkalizing vitamins and minerals, and cayenne to stimulate circulation and boost the detox, this is the ultimate jump-start to your day.

SERVES 2

¾ cup (180ml) coconut water or water

1 cup (37g) chopped romaine lettuce

1 medium tomato, chopped

1 medium carrot, diced

½ medium cucumber, chopped

1 medium avocado, pitted and peeled

1 lime, peeled and halved

1 clove garlic, peeled

¾ teaspoon natural salt, plus more to taste

Pinch of cayenne pepper

1½ cups (190g) ice cubes

OPTIONAL BOOSTERS

1 tablespoon cold-pressed extra-virgin olive oil

1 teaspoon chopped red onion

1 teaspoon Bragg liquid aminos

Throw all of the ingredients (except the ice cubes) into your blender and blast on high for about 1 minute, until smooth. Add more salt to taste, then add the ice cubes and blast for 10 to 20 seconds more, until well combined.

NUTRITIONAL FACTS (PER SERVING)

CALORIES 209 KCAL | FAT 15 G | SATURATED FAT 2 G | SODIUM 914 MG | CARBS 20 G | FIBER 10 G | SUGARS 5 G
PROTEIN 3 G | CALCIUM 64 MG | IRON 1 MG

spicy wake-up!

 IMMUNITY DETOX WEIGHT LOSS ALKALINE UNSWEETENED

Strawberries and red bell pepper blend up a taste sensation. Boost with cayenne for even more heat and a dose of capsaicin, a natural antibiotic that reduces inflammation. Packed with vitamins A, C, and E (camu powder and broccoli boosters add even more), this mocktail wards off the nasties while keeping your skin and hair gorgeous. It's my immunity idol.

SERVES 2

1½ cups (360ml) coconut water or water, plus more as needed

½ cup (120ml) unfiltered apple juice

¼ cup (35g) diced red bell pepper

3 cups (480g) frozen strawberries

5 drops alcohol-free liquid stevia, plus more to taste (optional)

OPTIONAL BOOSTERS

1 teaspoon camu powder

¼ cup (30g) frozen raw broccoli florets

Pinch of cayenne pepper

Throw all of the ingredients into your blender and blast on high for about 1 minute, until smooth and creamy. Add more water as needed to blend. Tweak sweetener to taste.

NUTRITIONAL FACTS (PER SERVING)

CALORIES 110 KCAL | FAT 0 G | SATURATED FAT 0 G | SODIUM 12 MG | CARBS 26 G | FIBER 5 G | SUGARS 18 G
PROTEIN 1 G | CALCIUM 49 MG | IRON 1 MG

strawberry heat

IMMUNITY   DETOX   WEIGHT LOSS   UNSWEETENED

Carrot, apple, and lemon are a classic combination in juices and smoothies. These immunity-boosting stars, coupled with the warming, anti-inflammatory properties of ginger and cinnamon, make this blend a powerful cold-and-flu buster. Add the cayenne for a fiery punch!

SERVES 2

1½ cups (360ml) water

2 medium carrots, diced (grated, if using a conventional blender)

1 green apple, skin on, cored and chopped

2 teaspoons freshly squeezed lemon juice

2 teaspoons minced ginger

¼ teaspoon ground cinnamon

1½ cups (240g) frozen mango

OPTIONAL BOOSTERS

Pinch of cayenne pepper

1 tablespoon flaxseed oil

1 tablespoon goji powder

Throw the water, carrots, and apple into your blender and start out on low until the apple and carrots have broken down. Turn your blender to high and blast for about 1 minute, until well combined. Add the remaining ingredients and blend on high for 10 to 20 seconds more, until smooth and creamy.

NUTRITIONAL FACTS (PER SERVING)

CALORIES 147 KCAL | FAT 0 G | SATURATED FAT 0 G | SODIUM 51 MG | CARBS 37 G | FIBER 6 G | SUGARS 28 G
PROTEIN 1 G | CALCIUM 48 MG | IRON 0 MG

strength

INFLAMMATION   IMMUNITY   DETOX   WEIGHT LOSS   UNSWEETENED

Be bold and boost this summer smoothie into a delicious curry! Packed with anti-inflammatory power, digestive support, and cleansing magic (all virtues of red pepper flakes and yellow curry spices), this is a fabulous winter warmer.

SERVES 2

1 1/2 cups (360ml) coconut water or water

1/2 cup (125ml) canned coconut milk (shake, then pour)

3/4 teaspoon finely grated lime zest, plus more to taste

1/8 teaspoon natural salt

1 cup (160g) frozen mango

1 cup (160g) frozen pineapple

1 cup (160g) frozen peaches

Natural sweetener (optional)

OPTIONAL BOOSTERS

1/2 teaspoon yellow curry powder

1/8 teaspoon red pepper flakes, plus more to taste

1 tablespoon avocado oil

Throw all of the ingredients into your blender and blast on high for 30 to 60 seconds, until smooth and creamy. Tweak flavors to taste (you may want more lime zest or sweetener).

NUTRITIONAL FACTS (PER SERVING)

CALORIES 230 KCAL | FAT 12 G | SATURATED FAT 10 G | SODIUM 161 MG | CARBS 31 G | FIBER 3 G | SUGARS 25 G PROTEIN 2 G | CALCIUM 40 MG | IRON 2 MG

tropical crush or curry

INFLAMMATION   ENERGIZING   DETOX   UNSWEETENED

If you love green tea ice cream, then you'll go crazy for this blend. (If you don't, this one ain't for you!) Compounds in green tea have powerful antioxidant properties—greater than vitamins C and E. This is not the prettiest smoothie, but boy is it delicious.

SERVES 2

2 green tea bags

2 1/4 cups (540ml) boiling water

1/4 cup (7g) loosely packed baby spinach

1/2 cup (110g) silken tofu

1/2 medium avocado, pitted and peeled

1 cup (170g) chopped pitted dates, soaked (see page 6)

1 teaspoon natural vanilla extract

1 cup (125g) ice cubes

OPTIONAL BOOSTERS

1 tablespoon raw unsalted cashews, soaked (see page 6)

1 teaspoon shelled hemp seeds

1 teaspoon chia seeds

In a small bowl, steep the tea bags in the boiling water for 30 to 60 seconds. Remove the bags, allow the tea to cool, and refrigerate until fully chilled.

Pour the tea into your blender and throw in the rest of the ingredients (except the ice cubes). Blast on high for 30 to 60 seconds, until well combined. Add the ice cubes and blast for about 10 seconds more, until combined.

NUTRITIONAL FACTS (PER SERVING)

CALORIES 361 KCAL | FAT 9 G | SATURATED FAT 1 G | SODIUM 27 MG | CARBS 69 G | FIBER 9 G | SUGARS 57 G PROTEIN 7 G | CALCIUM 184 MG | IRON 2 MG

green tea ice cream

PROTEIN RICH   **ENERGIZING**

Sweet and buttery, with an exquisite hint of cardamom, this will seduce your taste buds while lowering cholesterol, scouring toxins in the colon, and reducing belly-fat stores. Vitamins C and A in both fruits make for an awesome anti-ager!

SERVES 2

1 cup (240ml) freshly squeezed orange juice

2 ripe pears, skin on, cored and chopped

2 cups (320g) frozen blueberries

Pinch of ground cardamom, plus more to taste

OPTIONAL BOOSTERS

2 teaspoons maqui powder

¼ cup (30g) frozen raw broccoli florets

1 tablespoon flaxseed oil

Throw all of the ingredients into your blender and blast on high for 30 to 60 seconds, until smooth and creamy. Tweak cardamom to taste.

NUTRITIONAL FACTS (PER SERVING)

CALORIES 147 KCAL | FAT 0 G | SATURATED FAT 0 G | SODIUM 2 MG | CARBS 36 G | FIBER 4 G | SUGARS 26 G PROTEIN 2 G | CALCIUM 23 MG | IRON 0 MG

pear it with blue

INFLAMMATION   ENERGIZING   IMMUNITY   DETOX   UNSWEETENED

Pie devotees: get your pie fix faster than you can preheat the oven. The boosters ramp up the nutrition without altering taste, and the cashews add a rich, buttery pastry flavor. Soak those nuts for a creamy shake reminiscent of that perfect bite à la mode.

SERVES 2

¾ cup (180ml) unsweetened almond milk (strained if homemade)

1¾ cups (475g) unsweetened applesauce or stewed apples

1 cup (140g) raw unsalted cashews, soaked (see page 6)

2 teaspoons natural vanilla extract, plus more to taste

¾ teaspoon ground cinnamon, plus more to taste

2 chopped, pitted, and soaked dates (see page 6), or 1 tablespoon pure maple syrup, plus more to taste

1 cup (125g) ice cubes

OPTIONAL BOOSTERS

1 tablespoon lucuma powder

1 cup (43g) firmly packed baby spinach

½ cup (60g) frozen raw cauliflower florets

Throw all of the ingredients (except the ice cubes) into your blender and blast on high for 30 to 60 seconds, until smooth and creamy. Add the ice cubes and blast for 10 to 20 seconds more, until well combined. Tweak flavors to taste (you may want to add more vanilla, cinnamon, or sweetener).

NUTRITIONAL FACTS (PER SERVING)

CALORIES 567 KCAL | FAT 32 G | SATURATED FAT 5 G | SODIUM 70 MG | CARBS 63 G | FIBER 9 G | SUGARS 36 G | PROTEIN 13 G | CALCIUM 226 MG | IRON 5 MG

apple pie in a glass

PROTEIN RICH   **CONTAINS NUTS**   **ENERGIZING**

Chocoholics beware—this one is addictive. Oats, cashews, almond butter, and pecans create a flavor similar to the most decadent bowl of brownie batter. Don't miss the peppermint booster for a Thin Mint homage that should earn any Girl Scout a merit badge.

SERVES 2

2 cups (480ml) unsweetened almond milk or other nut, grain, or seed milk (strained if homemade)

3 tablespoons raw cacao powder or unsweetened cocoa powder

1/4 cup (22g) rolled oats

1/2 cup (70g) raw unsalted cashews, soaked (see page 6)

2 tablespoons raw pecans, soaked (see page 6)

2 tablespoons raw almond butter

1 teaspoon natural vanilla extract

1 tablespoon pure maple syrup, plus more to taste

1 1/2 medium frozen sliced bananas

1/2 cup (62g) ice cubes

OPTIONAL BOOSTERS

1/4 teaspoon peppermint extract

1 tablespoon açaí powder

1/4 cup (30g) frozen raw cauliflower florets

Throw all of the ingredients (except the frozen bananas and ice cubes) into your blender and blast on high for 30 to 60 seconds, until the nuts are completely pureed. Add the bananas and ice cubes and blast for 10 to 20 seconds more, until smooth and creamy.

NUTRITIONAL FACTS (PER SERVING)

CALORIES 570 KCAL | FAT 33 G SATURATED FAT 4 G | SODIUM 162 MG | CARBS 61 G | FIBER 10 G | SUGARS 27 G PROTEIN 15 G | CALCIUM 556 MG | IRON 5 MG

brownie batter

PROTEIN RICH   CONTAINS NUTS   ENERGIZING

A liquid equivalent of the classic dessert favorite, this retake is decadent and creamy (if you soak the cashews), and doesn't fall "short" of its baked counterpart. Just try to resist this fabulous and fun shake.

SERVES 2

1 3/4 cups (420ml) water

3/4 cup (105g) raw unsalted cashews, soaked (see page 6)

1 tablespoon natural vanilla extract

1/4 cup (43g) chopped pitted dates, soaked (see page 6)

2 tablespoons pure maple syrup

2 cups (320g) frozen strawberries

OPTIONAL BOOSTERS

1 teaspoon pomegranate powder

1 teaspoon flaxseed oil

1 teaspoon goji powder

Throw all of the ingredients into your blender and blast on high for about 1 minute, until smooth and creamy.

NUTRITIONAL FACTS (PER SERVING)

CALORIES 471 KCAL | FAT 23 G | SATURATED FAT 4 G | SODIUM 19 MG | CARBS 58 G | FIBER 6 G | SUGARS 38 G PROTEIN 11 G | CALCIUM 86 MG | IRON 4 MG

strawberry shortcake

PROTEIN RICH   **CONTAINS NUTS**   **ENERGIZING**

This is an indulgence that makes no apologies—it's way too good. Lemon and poppy seeds party in the brilliant batter blended up with almonds, cashews, and oats. Add more lemon zest for zing, and boost with protein powder for richness, and cauliflower and chia to stave off pangs of greedy guilt.

SERVES 2

1¾ cups (420ml) unsweetened almond milk or other nut, grain, or seed milk (strained if homemade)

½ cup (70g) raw unsalted cashews, soaked (see page 6)

⅓ cup (30g) rolled oats

1 teaspoon natural vanilla extract

½ teaspoon finely grated lemon zest, plus more to taste

2 tablespoons freshly squeezed lemon juice, plus more to taste

¼ cup (43g) chopped pitted dates, soaked (see page 6)

2 teaspoons poppy seeds

1 medium frozen sliced banana

1 cup (125g) ice cubes

OPTIONAL BOOSTERS

1 tablespoon vanilla protein powder

¼ cup (30g) frozen raw cauliflower florets

1 tablespoon chia seeds

Throw all of the ingredients (except the poppy seeds, frozen banana, and ice cubes) into your blender and blast on high for 30 to 60 seconds, until creamy. Throw in the poppy seeds, frozen banana, and ice cubes and blast for about 10 seconds more, until smooth. Tweak lemon zest and juice to taste.

NUTRITIONAL FACTS (PER SERVING)

CALORIES 439 KCAL | FAT 19 G | SATURATED FAT 3 G | SODIUM 141 MG | CARBS 59 G | FIBER 7 G | SUGARS 30 G PROTEIN 10 G | CALCIUM 476 MG | IRON 4 MG

lemon–poppy seed muffin

PROTEIN RICH   **CONTAINS NUTS**   **ENERGIZING**

The magical combination of these ingredients produces a decadent flavor that tastes just like a freshly baked loaf of banana bread. Add the olive oil, coconut, pecans, and a half nana for an even richer experience. This dessert smoothie is deliberately thick. Glug or devour it with a spoon—just don't miss it!

SERVES 2

2 cups (480ml) unsweetened almond milk (strained if homemade)

1 medium avocado, pitted and peeled

3 tablespoons pure maple syrup

1 teaspoon natural vanilla extract

Pinch of ground cinnamon, plus more to taste

½ medium frozen sliced banana, plus more to taste

1½ cups (190g) ice cubes

OPTIONAL BOOSTERS

1 teaspoon cold-pressed extra-virgin olive oil

1 teaspoon shredded unsweetened coconut

1 tablespoon raw pecans, soaked (see page 6)

Throw all of the ingredients into your blender and blast on high for 30 to 60 seconds, until smooth and creamy. Tweak banana to taste.

NUTRITIONAL FACTS (PER SERVING)

CALORIES 331 KCAL | FAT 17 G | SATURATED FAT 2 G | SODIUM 166 MG | CARBS 43 G | FIBER 8 G | SUGARS 29 G
PROTEIN 3 G | CALCIUM 499 MG | IRON 1 MG

avo-nana bread

ENERGIZING   CONTAINS NUTS

A healthy chocolate fix that helps you relax and feel good? Yes, please. The cherries contains quercetin, ellagic acid, and perillyl alcohol—potent anticancer agents. The anthocyanins and bioflavonoids in cherries act like aspirin and ibuprofen to help eliminate migraines without the side effects, and the antioxidant melatonin promotes sleep.

SERVES 2

1½ cups (360ml) coconut water or water

1 tablespoon raw cacao powder or unsweetened cocoa powder

¼ cup (6g) torn-up beet greens (1 large leaf with stalk removed)

2 tablespoons raw unsalted cashews, soaked (see page 6)

1 tablespoon plain or vanilla–flavored yogurt

1 teaspoon natural vanilla extract

1 teaspoon freshly squeezed lemon juice

2 chopped pitted dates, soaked (see page 6)

⅛ teaspoon ground cinnamon

2½ cups (350g) frozen pitted sweet cherries

½ medium frozen sliced banana

OPTIONAL BOOSTERS

1 tablespoon chia seeds

1 teaspoon açaí powder

1 teaspoon flaxseed oil

Throw all of the ingredients into your blender and blast on high for about 1 minute, until smooth and creamy.

NUTRITIONAL FACTS (PER SERVING)

CALORIES 171 KCAL | FAT 5 G | SATURATED FAT 0 G | SODIUM 30 MG | CARBS 31 G | FIBER 8 G | SUGARS 19 G PROTEIN 2 G | CALCIUM 49 MG | IRON 1 MG

black forest cake

ENERGIZING   CONTAINS NUTS

This tastes like a Pop-Tart, and is great for digestive health. Oats are a wonderful source of fiber, to combat carcinogens in the gastrointestinal tract. And both oats and blueberries become gelatinous in the colon, helping to expel toxins and lower blood pressure and cholesterol.

SERVES 2

2 ¼ cups (540ml) unsweetened almond milk, hemp milk, or rice milk (strained if homemade)

⅓ cup (45g) raw unsalted cashews, soaked (see page 6)

⅓ cup (30g) rolled oats

2 tablespoons pure maple syrup, plus more to taste

1 tablespoon chia seeds

½ teaspoon ground cinnamon

2 cups (320g) frozen blueberries

OPTIONAL BOOSTERS

1 tablespoon maqui powder

1 tablespoon ground flaxseeds

1 teaspoon coconut oil

Throw the milk, cashews, and oats into your blender and blast on high for 30 to 60 seconds, until creamy. Add the remaining ingredients and blast again on high for about 20 seconds, until smooth. Tweak the maple syrup to taste.

NUTRITIONAL FACTS (PER SERVING)

CALORIES 415 KCAL | FAT 15 G | SATURATED FAT 2 G | SODIUM 178 MG | CARBS 64 G | FIBER 9 G | SUGARS 37 G PROTEIN 9 G | CALCIUM 588 MG | IRON 3 MG

blueberry breakfast tart

PROTEIN RICH   **CONTAINS NUTS**   **ENERGIZING**

Inspired by a famous blend at my favorite local restaurant, SunCafe, this spectacular green goddess is the most popular recipe on my website and in *The Blender Girl* cookbook. I receive hundreds of emails a week from recovering greenophobes proclaiming this the Holy Grail of Kale.

SERVES 2

2 cups (480ml) water
Serves 2 1/2 cup (70g) raw
unsalted cashews, soaked
(see page 6)

1 cup (25g) torn-up curly green
kale leaves (1 or 2 large leaves
with stalk removed), plus
more to taste

2 sliced medium ripe bananas

1/4 cup (43g) chopped pitted
dates, soaked (see page 6),
or 1 tablespoon pure maple
syrup, plus more to taste

1/2 teaspoon natural vanilla
extract

1/2 teaspoon minced ginger,
plus more to taste

1 cup (125g) ice cubes

OPTIONAL BOOSTERS

1 tablespoon shelled hemp
seeds

1 tablespoon flaxseed oil

1 tablespoon chia seeds

Throw all of the ingredients (except the ice cubes) into your blender and puree on high for about 1 minute, until smooth and creamy. Add the ice cubes and blast for 10 to 20 seconds more, until well combined. Tweak flavors to taste (you may like a bit more kale, sweetener, or ginger).

NUTRITIONAL FACTS (PER SERVING)

CALORIES 386 KCAL | FAT 15 G | SATURATED FAT 2 G | SODIUM 23 MG | CARBS 60 G | FIBER 6 G | SUGARS 35 G
PROTEIN 8 G | CALCIUM 62 MG | IRON 3 MG

tastes-like-ice-cream kale

PROTEIN RICH   **CONTAINS NUTS**   **ENERGIZING**

Repeat after me: "Pecans are full of fiber, protein, and healthy unsaturated fats that may lower cholesterol." That should stave off the guilt while you blend up dessert. Throw in the cauliflower, hemp seeds, and flaxseed oil and this becomes a nutrient-boosting hero behind a mask of indulgence.

SERVES 2

1½ cups (360ml) water

1 cup (110g) raw pecans, soaked (see page 6)

3 tablespoons pure maple syrup

1 tablespoon natural vanilla extract

½ teaspoon ground cinnamon

2 medium frozen sliced bananas

1 cup (125g) ice cubes

OPTIONAL BOOSTERS

½ cup (60g) frozen raw cauliflower florets

1 tablespoon shelled hemp seeds

1 tablespoon flaxseed oil

Throw all of the ingredients into your blender and blast on high for 30 to 60 seconds, until smooth and creamy.

NUTRITIONAL FACTS (PER SERVING)

CALORIES 583 KCAL | FAT 40 G | SATURATED FAT 3 G | SODIUM 15 MG | CARBS 56 G | FIBER 8 G | SUGARS 35 G
PROTEIN 6 G | CALCIUM 89 MG | IRON 1 MG

pecan pie

PROTEIN RICH   CONTAINS NUTS   ENERGIZING

A star from *The Blender Girl* cookbook, this decadent dessert shake tastes just like a melted raspberry cheesecake. But soak those nuts for ultimate creaminess! And don't forget the boosters: the coconut gives an exotic twist, the pomegranate adds antioxidants, and the chile spices things up!

SERVES 2

1½ cups (360ml) coconut water or water

¾ cup (105g) raw unsalted cashews, soaked (see page 6)

½ medium sliced banana

3 tablespoons freshly squeezed lemon juice, plus more to taste

1 tablespoon pure maple syrup, plus more to taste

1 teaspoon natural vanilla extract

Pinch of finely grated lemon zest, plus more to taste

Pinch of natural salt (optional, to bring out flavors)

1½ cups (240g) frozen raspberries

1 cup (125g) ice cubes

OPTIONAL BOOSTERS

1 tablespoon coconut oil

1 tablespoon pomegranate powder

½ teaspoon finely chopped serrano chile

Throw all of the ingredients into your blender and blast on high for about 1 minute, until smooth and creamy. Tweak flavors to taste (you may like a bit more lemon juice, sweetener, or zest).

NUTRITIONAL FACTS (PER SERVING)

Calories 415 kcal | **Fat** 23 g | **Saturated fat** 4 g | **Sodium** 93 mg | **Carbs** 45 g | **Fiber** 10 g | **Sugars** 18 g **Protein** 11 g | **Calcium** 69 mg | **Iron** 4 mg

raspberry-lemon cheesecake

PROTEIN RICH   CONTAINS NUTS   ENERGIZING

If the world were ending, I'd make this decadent treat my finale. The incredible creaminess and blend of warm spices will make you weak in the knees. The boosters add an injection of protein and omega-3s—so you may feel a tad less cheeky as you head to heaven.

SERVES 2

1 cup (240ml) unsweetened almond milk or other nut, grain, or seed milk (strained if homemade)

1 cup (240ml) coconut water

¼ cup (43g) chopped pitted dates, soaked (see page 6)

1 teaspoon natural vanilla extract

½ teaspoon ground cinnamon

¼ teaspoon ground ginger

⅛ teaspoon ground nutmeg

⅛ teaspoon ground cardamom

Pinch of ground cloves

Pinch of natural salt (optional, to bring out flavors)

2 medium frozen sliced bananas

1 cup (125g) ice cubes (optional)

OPTIONAL BOOSTERS

1 tablespoon blanched raw almonds, soaked (see page 6)

1 tablespoon chia seeds

1 tablespoon flaxseed oil

Throw all of the ingredients into your blender and puree on high for 30 to 60 seconds, until smooth and creamy.

NUTRITIONAL FACTS (PER SERVING)

CALORIES 227 KCAL | FAT 1 G | SATURATED FAT 0 G | SODIUM 280 MG | CARBS 52 G | FIBER 6 G | SUGARS 35 G | PROTEIN 3 G | CALCIUM 284 MG | IRON 1 MG

chai tai

ENERGIZING   **CONTAINS NUTS**

Disguised as an everyday chocolate milkshake—but hiding all manner of nutritious goodies—this blend is a fun way to sneak veggies into kids. If you can't embrace blending wet florets, add an extra banana and reduce the sweetener. Grown-ups: a pinch of cayenne kicks this into "wow!"

SERVES 2

1¼ cups (300ml) unsweetened soy, rice, hemp, or almond milk (strained if homemade)

½ cup (22g) firmly packed baby spinach

¼ cup (25g) frozen raw broccoli florets

1 medium sliced banana, plus more to taste

½ ripe pear, cored, plus more to taste

1 cup (120g) steamed cauliflower florets (cooled completely), or an extra sliced banana (to save time if you don't have a bit of leftover cauliflower)

2 tablespoons raw cacao powder or unsweetened cocoa powder, plus more to taste

2 teaspoons natural vanilla extract

3 tablespoons pure maple syrup, plus more to taste

1 cup (125g) ice cubes

OPTIONAL BOOSTERS

1 tablespoon shelled hemp seeds

1 tablespoon açaí powder

Pinch of cayenne pepper

Throw all of the ingredients into your blender and blast on high for 30 to 60 seconds, until smooth and creamy. Tweak flavors to taste (you may like a bit more banana, pear, cacao, vanilla, or maple syrup).

NUTRITIONAL FACTS (PER SERVING)

CALORIES 240 KCAL | FAT 2 G | SATURATED FAT 0 G | SODIUM 133 MG | CARBS 53 G | FIBER 7 G | SUGARS 36 G
PROTEIN 4 G | CALCIUM 358 MG | IRON 2 MG

chock-full chocolate surprise

ENERGIZING

Powerful antioxidants (from the sweet spud's beta-carotene and vitamins A and C) make this shake an immune-boosting alternative to baked pie. Fortify it with boosters to balance the indulgence. Loaded with fiber, this smoothie rocks, and I don't mind sayin' it. Who eats humble pie anyway?

SERVES 2

1¼ cups (300ml) unsweetened rice milk or other nut, grain, or seed milk (strained if homemade)

1½ cups (385g) mashed cooked orange sweet potato

3 tablespoons pure maple syrup

1 teaspoon natural vanilla extract

½ teaspoon ground cinnamon

¼ teaspoon ground ginger

¼ teaspoon ground nutmeg

Pinch of natural salt (optional, to bring out flavors)

1 medium frozen sliced banana

1 cup (125g) ice cubes

OPTIONAL BOOSTERS

1 tablespoon shelled hemp seeds

1 tablespoon flaxseed oil

1 teaspoon goji powder

Throw all of the ingredients into your blender and blast on high for 30 to 60 seconds, until smooth and creamy.

NUTRITIONAL FACTS (PER SERVING)

CALORIES 376 KCAL | FAT 1 G | SATURATED FAT 0 G | SODIUM 246 MG | CARBS 87 G | FIBER 8 G | SUGARS 41 G
PROTEIN 4 G | CALCIUM 277 MG | IRON 1 MG

sweet potato pie

ENERGIZING

IMMUNITY

A healthy blend of luxury, this delivers all of the essential amino acids via the beet greens. It's also high in tryptophan (key for the production of serotonin), which helps regulate mood and sleep cycles. Cook your beet roots, or your treat may taste like it's been playing in the dirt.

SERVES 2

1¼ cups (300ml) rice milk or other nut, grain, or seed milk (strained if homemade)

½ cup (12g) torn-up beet greens (1 or 2 large leaves with stalk removed)

3 small or 2 medium red beets, baked (but not roasted) until soft

½ medium sliced banana

3 tablespoons raw cacao powder or unsweetened cocoa powder, plus more to taste

1 tablespoon pure maple syrup, plus more to taste

½ teaspoon natural vanilla extract

1 cup (160g) frozen mixed berries

1 cup (125g) ice cubes

OPTIONAL BOOSTERS

1 tablespoon chia seeds

1 tablespoon maqui powder

1 teaspoon flaxseed oil

Throw all of the ingredients into your blender and blast on high for 30 to 60 seconds, until smooth and creamy. Tweak the cacao and sweetener to taste.

NUTRITIONAL FACTS (PER SERVING)

CALORIES 224 KCAL | FAT 3 G | SATURATED FAT 0 G | SODIUM 136 MG | CARBS 51 G | FIBER 7 G | SUGARS 31 G
PROTEIN 4 G | CALCIUM 224 MG | IRON 2 MG

can't beet red velvet cake

ENERGIZING

Sometimes you just need a treat, and this one is pure indulgence. Soak the cashews and coconut for the best results, and throw in the healthy boosters, lest you be attacked by pangs of guilt. Blend your way to bliss, and thank me later.

SERVES 2

1½ cups (360ml) coconut water or water

½ cup (50g) shredded unsweetened coconut

¼ cup (35g) raw unsalted cashews, soaked (see page 6)

1 teaspoon pure maple syrup (optional)

1 teaspoon natural vanilla extract

2 large ripe bananas, sliced and frozen

1½ cups (190g) ice cubes

OPTIONAL BOOSTERS

1 cup (43g) firmly packed baby spinach

1 tablespoon coconut oil

1 tablespoon shelled hemp seeds

Throw all of the ingredients into your blender and blast on high for 30 to 60 seconds, until smooth and creamy.

NUTRITIONAL FACTS (PER SERVING)

CALORIES 397 KCAL | FAT 24 G | SATURATED FAT 15 G | SODIUM 24 MG | CARBS 44 G | FIBER 8 G | SUGARS 21 G
PROTEIN 6 G | CALCIUM 31 MG | IRON 2 MG

banana-coconut cream pie

PROTEIN RICH   **CONTAINS NUTS**   **ENERGIZING**   **UNSWEETENED**

The healing power of peaches makes the nasties crumble: vitamin C scavenges free radicals and fights infection, beta-carotene converts to retinol for eye health, fatty acids help maintain healthy mucous membranes and skin elasticity, and potassium helps regulate heart rate and lower blood pressure. Or just enjoy the flavor.

SERVES 2

1 cup (240ml) freshly squeezed orange juice

1 cup (240ml) unsweetened almond milk, rice milk, or hemp milk (strained if homemade)

1/2 cup (44g) rolled oats

1/2 teaspoon natural vanilla extract

1 tablespoon raw unsalted cashews, soaked (see page 6)

1 tablespoon pure maple syrup

1/8 teaspoon ground cinnamon

1/2 medium frozen sliced banana

2 cups (320g) frozen peaches

OPTIONAL BOOSTERS

1 tablespoon plain or vanilla-flavored yogurt

1 tablespoon chia seeds

1 tablespoon flaxseed oil

Throw all of the ingredients into your blender and blast on high for 30 to 60 seconds, until smooth and creamy.

NUTRITIONAL FACTS (PER SERVING)

CALORIES 311 KCAL | FAT 5 G | SATURATED FAT 0 G | SODIUM 80 MG | CARBS 62 G | FIBER 6 G | SUGARS 37 G
PROTEIN 6 G | CALCIUM 275 MG | IRON 2 MG

peach crumble

PROTEIN RICH   CONTAINS NUTS   ENERGIZING

Omega-3 and -6 fatty acids are vital for building healthy cells; maintaining brain and nerve function; controlling blood clotting; and protecting against heart disease and stroke, arthritis, asthma, depression, and Alzheimer's. This blend combines all of the top plant-based sources of both (add the boosters!) in one scrumptious slurp.

SERVES 2

2 cups (480ml) unsweetened almond milk (strained if homemade)

1 medium banana

1 teaspoon chia seeds

1 teaspoon ground flaxseeds

1 teaspoon shelled hemp seeds

1/4 teaspoon ground cinnamon, plus more to taste

1 tablespoon pure maple syrup, plus more to taste

2 cups (320g) frozen mixed berries

OPTIONAL BOOSTERS

1 tablespoon açaí powder

1 tablespoon flaxseed oil

1/2 cup (15g) loosely packed chard leaves

Throw all of the ingredients into your blender and blast on high for about 1 minute, until smooth and creamy. Tweak cinnamon and maple syrup to taste.

NUTRITIONAL FACTS (PER SERVING)

CALORIES 256 KCAL | FAT 5 G | SATURATED FAT 0 G | SODIUM 155 MG | CARBS 52 G | FIBER 7 G | SUGARS 36 G
PROTEIN 4 G | CALCIUM 489 MG | IRON 1 MG

omega overture

PROTEIN RICH   CONTAINS NUTS   ENERGIZING   IMMUNITY

Quench those cravings with this decadent blend! The natural sweetness of carrot accented with pineapple, cashews, oats, and spices bring on the cake flavor, with yogurt and lemon for your cream cheese–frosting fix. Cauliflower and goji powder boost nutrition without altering taste, and walnuts add to the nutty adventure.

SERVES 2

2 cups (480ml) fresh carrot juice

½ teaspoon natural vanilla extract

1 teaspoon ground cinnamon

½ teaspoon ground nutmeg

½ teaspoon ground ginger

Tiny pinch of ground cloves

¾ cup (105g) raw unsalted cashews, soaked (see page 6)

¼ cup (22g) rolled oats

2 tablespoons plain or vanilla-flavored yogurt, plus more to taste

1 teaspoon freshly squeezed lemon juice, plus more to taste

1 teaspoon pure maple syrup, plus more to taste

¾ cup (120g) frozen pineapple

1 medium frozen sliced banana

OPTIONAL BOOSTERS

2 tablespoons raw walnuts, soaked (see page 6)

¼ cup (30g) frozen raw cauliflower florets

1 teaspoon goji powder

Throw all of the ingredients (except the frozen pineapple and banana) into your blender and blast on high for 30 to 60 seconds, until the nuts and oats are pureed. Add the frozen fruit and blast for 10 to 20 seconds more, until smooth and creamy.

NUTRITIONAL FACTS (PER SERVING)

CALORIES 537 KCAL | FAT 25 G | SATURATED FAT 4 G | SODIUM 171 MG | CARBS 71 G | FIBER 8 G | SUGARS 28 G | PROTEIN 14 G | CALCIUM 128 MG | IRON 5 MG

carrot cake

PROTEIN RICH　　**CONTAINS NUTS**　　**ENERGIZING**

This decadent dream is the ultimate mood enhancer: bananas aid serotonin and norepinephrine production. They also stimulate brain activity, replenish glycogen, and alleviate nausea, PMS, and stress. Potassium promotes heart health, fiber helps digestion, and magnesium strengthens bones. The vegetables boost nutrition without changing flavor, and cinnamon is the bomb!

SERVES 2

2 cups (480ml) unsweetened nut, grain, or seed milk (strained if homemade)

1/4 cup (43g) chopped pitted dates, soaked (see page 6)

1 teaspoon natural vanilla extract

3 medium frozen sliced bananas

OPTIONAL BOOSTERS

1/2 teaspoon ground cinnamon

1/2 cup (51g) chopped bok choy

1/4 cup (30g) frozen raw cauliflower florets

Throw all of the ingredients into your blender and blast on high for 30 to 60 seconds, until smooth and creamy.

NUTRITIONAL FACTS (PER SERVING)

CALORIES 327 KCAL | FAT 2 G | SATURATED FAT 0 G | SODIUM 92 MG | CARBS 74 G | FIBER 7 G | SUGARS 44 G
PROTEIN 6 G | CALCIUM 222 MG | IRON 1 MG

banana bomb

PROTEIN RICH   **ENERGIZING**

Sinfully rich and accented with subtle orange notes, this is inspired by a mind-blowing torte in *The Blender Girl* cookbook that brought chocaholics to the blender altar. Add the spinach, chia seeds, and maca powder to combat stress and boost energy, or just for crazy-good flavor.

SERVES 2

1½ cups (360ml) unsweetened almond or hemp milk (strained if homemade)

¼ cup (18g) raw cacao powder or unsweetened cocoa powder

½ teaspoon natural vanilla extract

2 chopped pitted dates, soaked (see page 6)

¼ teaspoon natural orange extract

3 medium frozen sliced bananas

1 cup (125g) ice cubes (optional)

OPTIONAL BOOSTERS

1 teaspoon maca powder

1 cup (43g) firmly packed baby spinach

1 tablespoon chia seeds

Throw all of the ingredients into your blender and blast on high for about 1 minute, until smooth and creamy.

NUTRITIONAL FACTS (PER SERVING)

CALORIES 346 KCAL | FAT 2 G | SATURATED FAT 0 G | SODIUM 73 MG | CARBS 82 G | FIBER 11 G | SUGARS 49 G PROTEIN 7 G | CALCIUM 191 MG | IRON 2 MG

choc-orange-nana

PROTEIN RICH   ENERGIZING

This immune-boosting dessert delivers probiotics and fiber to aid digestion, copper to bolster red blood cells, and your daily allowance of vitamin C. Compounds in the strawberries also neutralize cancer cells (specifically colon, cervical, breast, and prostate). Use any plain milk and yogurt, and boost it for healthy fatty acids and protein.

SERVES 2

1 1/2 cups (360ml) unsweetened almond milk, rice milk, or hemp milk (strained if homemade)

1 tablespoon pure maple syrup, plus more to taste

1 teaspoon natural vanilla extract

1 medium banana

1/2 cup (120g) plain or vanilla-flavored yogurt

2 cups (320g) frozen strawberries, plus more to taste

OPTIONAL BOOSTERS

1 teaspoon chia seeds

1 teaspoon shelled hemp seeds

1 teaspoon ground flaxseeds

Throw all of the ingredients into your blender and blast on high for about 1 minute, until smooth and creamy. Tweak the strawberries and maple syrup to taste.

NUTRITIONAL FACTS (PER SERVING)

CALORIES 214 KCAL | FAT 4 G | SATURATED FAT 1 G | SODIUM 144 MG | CARBS 40 G | FIBER 5 G | SUGARS 28 G | PROTEIN 4 G | CALCIUM 448 MG | IRON 1 MG

sweet-and-sour straw-nana

IMMUNITY   CONTAINS   ENERGIZING
            NUTS

This blend boosts workout performance and recovery. Maca powder (aka Peruvian ginseng) delivers phytonutrients, amino acids, calcium, iron, manganese, vitamin B12, and fatty acids for energy, endurance, and adrenal support. Maca's steroid-like compounds work with easily digested banana carbs and the proteins in almond butter to assist muscle recovery and replenish glycogen.

SERVES 2

2 cups (480ml) coconut water

1 teaspoon maca powder

1/2 cup (140g) raw almond butter

1 tablespoon chia seeds

3 medium frozen sliced bananas

OPTIONAL BOOSTERS

1 tablespoon vanilla protein powder

1 cup (27g) loosely packed baby spinach

1/4 teaspoon ground cinnamon

Throw all of the ingredients into your blender and blast on high for 30 to 60 seconds, until smooth and creamy.

NUTRITIONAL FACTS (PER SERVING)

CALORIES 654 KCAL | FAT 41 G | SATURATED FAT 3 G | SODIUM 259 MG | CARBS 64 G | FIBER 16 G | SUGARS 31 G
PROTEIN 19 G | CALCIUM 337 MG | IRON 3 MG

maca mojo

PROTEIN RICH

CONTAINS NUTS

ENERGIZING

UNSWEETENED

Delightfully creamy, with a magical combination of rose water and cardamom (said to be a potent aphrodisiac), this drink casts a sensational spell. Use any yogurt (I use coconut) and add lemon juice for your preferred level of tang.

SERVES 2

¾ cup (180ml) canned coconut milk (shake, then pour), or any milk or kefir

1 cup (240g) plain or vanilla-flavored yogurt

½ teaspoon ground cardamom

1 teaspoon pure distilled rose water

1 teaspoon freshly squeezed lemon juice, plus more to taste

1 chopped pitted date, soaked (see page 6), plus more to taste, or other natural sweetener

2 medium sliced bananas, fresh or frozen

2 cups (250g) ice cubes, plus more to serve

OPTIONAL BOOSTERS

½ cup (60g) frozen raw cauliflower florets

1 tablespoon raw unsalted cashews, soaked (see page 6)

1 tablespoon flaxseed oil

Throw all of the ingredients into your blender and blast on high for 30 to 60 seconds, until smooth and creamy. Tweak flavors to taste (you may like more lemon juice or sweetener).

NUTRITIONAL FACTS (PER SERVING)

CALORIES 390 KCAL | FAT 22 G | SATURATED FAT 18 G | SODIUM 77 MG | CARBS 47 G | FIBER 4 G | SUGARS 30 G | PROTEIN 7 G | CALCIUM 185 MG | IRON 3 MG

rose water–cardamom lassi

PROTEIN RICH   ENERGIZING

With the vitamin C power of oranges, kiwis, and strawberries combined with the probiotics in yogurt, this is a powerful immunity blend. Use any yogurt (I use coconut, but Greek yogurt works "s'blendedly"). And don't miss the basil, for an exotic twist. This really does taste like candy.

SERVES 2

1¼ cups (300ml) freshly squeezed orange juice

3 medium ripe kiwis, peeled and chopped

¾ cup (180g) plain or vanilla-flavored yogurt

2 cups (320g) frozen strawberries

OPTIONAL BOOSTERS

2 tablespoons finely chopped basil

1 teaspoon flaxseed oil

1 teaspoon camu powder

Throw all of the ingredients into your blender and blast on high for 30 to 60 seconds, until smooth and creamy.

NUTRITIONAL FACTS (PER SERVING)

CALORIES 238 KCAL | FAT 4 G | SATURATED FAT 1 G | SODIUM 47 MG | CARBS 47 G | FIBER 6 G | SUGARS 34 G
PROTEIN 6 G | CALCIUM 186 MG | IRON 1 MG

strawberry-kiwi candy

PROTEIN RICH   IMMUNITY   UNSWEETENED

This alkaline dessert shake calls up memories of pumpkin pie, but forgets the pumpkin, refined sugar, and most of the carbs. A beacon of hope for diabetics, cancer patients, or those on restricted diets, this smoothie is downright delicious for everybody. You'll need a specific type of stevia, but it's totally worth it.

SERVES 2

1 cup (240ml) fresh carrot juice, strained

1 cup (240ml) unsweetened almond milk or hemp milk (strained if homemade)

1 cup (180g) young Thai coconut meat

¼ cup (60g) raw almond butter

1 teaspoon alcohol-free vanilla extract

¾ teaspoon ground cinnamon

¼ teaspoon ground nutmeg

Pinch of ground ginger

30 drops Sweet Leaf English Toffee liquid stevia, plus more to taste

1 cup (125g) ice cubes, plus more to taste

OPTIONAL BOOSTERS

1 tablespoon goji powder

1 tablespoon avocado oil

1 tablespoon chia seeds

Throw all of the ingredients into your blender and blast on high for 30 to 60 seconds, until smooth and creamy. Tweak flavors to taste (you may like a bit more stevia or ice cubes).

NUTRITIONAL FACTS (PER SERVING)

CALORIES 637 KCAL | FAT 51 G | SATURATED FAT 30 G | SODIUM 156 MG | CARBS 37 G | FIBER 12 G | SUGARS 18 G
PROTEIN 14 G | CALCIUM 297 MG | IRON 3 MG

no-pumpkin pie

 PROTEIN RICH   **CONTAINS NUTS**   **UNSWEETENED**   **ALKALINE**

the smoothie pantry

Beyond fruits and vegetables, these are my essential smoothie ingredients. The tips for pairing flavors may help guide your choices when using the Build Your Smoothie chart on page 10 to create your own blends.

liquids

Some smoothies with high–water content base ingredients like melon, cucumber, and orange need little or no added liquid, but liquid is almost always an essential ingredient. Here are the best liquids for creating awesome smoothies.

water

Smoothies made with filtered water taste better and are better for you. Choose a filtration system that suits your needs and budget (see page 224 for recommendations). These recipes *will* work with unfiltered tap water, but as water quality varies greatly, your body may end up doing the filtering. Whatever water you use in your smoothies, you can alkalize it (and increase the healing potential) with pH drops. You can purchase these drops (containing sodium/potassium bicarbonate, sodium chloride, and/or sodium chlorite) at health food stores and online. However, while these drops increase pH, they don't filter or cleanse the water. Distilled water can aid with detoxification, but I don't recommend it for everyday consumption because it has been deionized and robbed of its minerals. Use filtered water to make your ice, too.

coconut water

After plain filtered water, young Thai coconut water is my go-to liquid for smoothies. (As a coconut matures, its sugar content increases and ascorbic acid content decreases.) Low in calories and carbohydrates, and almost fat free, coconut water adds a sweet and slightly nutty flavor and pairs well with most fruits and vegetables. A natural isotonic energy drink that's higher in hydrating electrolytes than most commercial products, coconut water is a magical health elixir that's alkalizing and cleansing, and boosts the function of the liver, thyroid, kidneys, and gallbladder.

The healthiest and most economical way to get the water is to crack open the husk and shell and utilize both the water and the meat. The easiest way to open a coconut is with the Coco Jack tool; see page 241. I jack coconuts by the dozen and freeze both the meat and the water. When freezing the water, leave about 1 inch (2.5cm) at the top of the container to allow for expansion. Buy organic coconuts whenever possible, to avoid bleach and other toxic preservatives that prevent mold but contaminate the meat and water.

When purchasing commercially packed coconut water, look for organic, raw, and unpasteurized brands without additives or preservatives. Harmless Harvest and Exotic Superfoods (see page 241) offer pure raw coconut water that has not been heated and retains all of its live enzymes. Long-life varieties packed in cartons and bottles are basically just sugar water, devoid of real nutrients.

You can use plain filtered water as a substitute in any of the recipes. If you're allergic to coconut water, try maple water, cactus water, or olive water (see page 241).

juices

Unsweetened juices give smoothies awesome flavor and texture. Carrot, orange, grapefruit, apple, tangerine, grape, cranberry, pomegranate, lemon, and lime juices figure prominently in these recipes. When I can, I make fresh juices with raw ingredients.

Citrus juices are fast and easy to make with a basic juice press. Other juices call for a masticating or centrifugal juicer, or a blender (which often requires adding water to the basic ingredients, and straining). Raw juices are nutrient-dense and contain live enzymes for digestion and health. Use them immediately, right after juicing, to reduce degradation of nutrients.

In choosing commercial juices, go for pure and unsweetened: freshly squeezed orange, tangerine, grapefruit, and carrot juices; unfiltered apple juice; and pure grape, cranberry, and pomegranate juices. (My picks are on page 241.) Don't use long-life lemon or lime juices in unrefrigerated bottles; they taste terrible, and frozen natural options are so much better. For more exotic blends, try superfood juices like açaí, goji, noni, mangosteen, and sea buckthorn (see the resources section on page 241). Freeze leftover juice in ice cube trays; flavored ice (see note on page 223) makes a fantastic booster!

green tea and other teas

Green tea tastes great paired with citrus, sweet fruits like grapes and pineapple, and herbs like mint. Steep your tea lightly to avoid bitterness. Packed with vitamins, minerals, potent anti-inflammatories and immunity boosters, green tea is an excellent source of antioxidants and alkaloids, making it a great anti-aging tonic. A cup of green tea can help cleanse the kidneys, promote heart health, heighten mental clarity, and reduce the risk of stroke. Green tea is a terrific fat burner, too, so it makes a great addition to weight-loss blends.

I've used green tea sparingly in these recipes, but you can use a variety of other teas in smoothies with great results. Chamomile and rooibos pair well with peach, banana, and strawberry, and rooibos is delicious with blueberry as well. Black tea is magic with berries or banana and mango, and chai and yerba mate are both incredible blended with yogurt and banana. Because some nonorganically grown green teas contain high levels of fluoride, lead, and aluminum, purchase organic varieties if possible. See page 244 for a list of my favorite tea purveyors.

aloe vera juice

The sharp, clean flavor of aloe vera works well with citrus and sweet fruits like berries, peaches, and pineapples. For use in smoothies, purchase pure, unsweetened aloe vera juice, preferably organic and processed specifically for human consumption. Just ¼ cup (60ml) is a wonderful supplement for weight loss, detox, digestion, and immunity. However, consume aloe and aloe products in moderation, because large amounts can cause diarrhea, cramping, and dehydration.

Aloe's powerful antibacterial, antiviral, and antifungal properties boost immunity and cleanse the body of toxins and pathogens. The plant's juice contains leaf pulp that is rich in nutrients, fiber, and a natural laxative (anthraquinone), which can help keep you regular. Aloe also eases inflammation in the gut and can help heal ulcers in the stomach and intestines. As aloe improves circulation, regulates blood pressure and cholesterol, and reduces inflammation as well, it's great for promoting heart health and alleviating symptoms of rheumatoid arthritis. It's fantastic for radiant skin, too. See page 241 for my preferred brands.

milks

Each "milk" contributes its own flavor and texture to a smoothie. For nutrient diversity, taste bud satisfaction, and to keep things interesting, I use a variety. Currently the most widely available plant-based milks are almond, hemp, rice, soy, and coconut, so they appear most often in these recipes. But oat, hazelnut, cashew, macadamia, pecan, pistachio, sunflower seed, pumpkin seed, sesame seed, sacha inchi seed, flaxseed, millet, and quinoa milks make brilliant additions to shakes, too. If you're using commercial milks, look for unsweetened products with limited additives and preservatives.

Dairy milk can be substituted (and has been tested) in these recipes with spectacular results. However, when coconut milk is called for, it's nonnegotiable and shouldn't be substituted, because it alone delivers coconutty flavor. These recipes are built around canned coconut milk. (For uniform taste and texture, shake then pour.) With cartoned, add ½ cup (120ml) more to the recipe to get a taste as rich as canned. The mild flavor and creamy texture of almond milk makes it my preferred choice for smoothies because it blends well with most ingredients. If nut allergies are an issue, soy milk is a creamy alternative. Hemp milk, while creamy, is more assertive, and in large amounts can taste grassy. Rice milk is especially mild and a great option if multiple food allergies come into account, but it's watery and low in nutrition.

I blend up my own milks (using nuts, seeds, and grains and water) whenever possible. These raw milks contain live enzymes and nutrients, and are free of additives, preservatives, and hormones. You can completely control the integrity of your milk—the quality of the ingredients (I use organic, non-GMO), as well as the sugar levels, and texture. Another bonus is that your milks (unlike commercial milks) can be made more digestible by soaking your base ingredients (see page 6).

When making milks for smoothies, nix the sweetener and strain for the creamiest texture. You can use fibrous unstrained milks in your shakes, but you'll get some grit. In general, a one-to-three ratio (by volume) of food to water yields good results for unsweetened homemade milks. (The exception is flaxseeds, which absorb a lot of water.) For rich milks, I start with half of the water called for and gradually add more to get the taste and consistency I like. To learn more about making a variety of plant-based milks, check out my first book, *The Blender Girl*.

flavored ice

Pour leftover fruit or vegetable juice, nut milk, or tea into ice cube trays and freeze for a quick flavor or textural enhancer. My favorites are: coconut, almond, macadamia, and cashew milks; pineapple, apple, carrot, and spinach juices; herbal teas like chamomile and peppermint; green tea; and fresh herbs like basil and mint frozen in water. Flavored ices (especially if the ingredients have a high fat or sugar content) are softer than ice made from water and will melt more quickly.

greens

Loaded with nutrients, fiber, and antioxidants, greens oxygenate the cells and blood; boost immunity; alkalize and detoxify the body; reduce inflammation; combat disease and infection; promote healthy skin, nails, and hair; and act as prebiotics to encourage the proliferation of friendly bacteria, keeping the body in balance. I buy Earthbound Farm (see page 243) organic greens, which are always high in quality.

Ease into the green smoothie experience gradually and train your taste buds. Start with fruit-based blends with small amounts of mild leafy greens, then reduce the fruit and increase the vegetables. Try the mild greens first, then go to the medium, and graduate to the strong ones. Don't discount wild edibles. Grasses, lamb's-quarter, hibiscus, nasturtiums, and other forage provide an incredible opportunity to add nutritional diversity to your diet. Start with very small amounts, and add to taste.

spinach (mild)

With a mild taste that's easily masked by fruits and vegetables, spinach is my go-to choice for introductory green smoothies. A cup or two (30 to 60g) of baby leaves (full-grown are earthier) go into any blend without altering its flavor profile. Choose leaves that are crisp and vibrantly green. Spinach is a nutritional powerhouse with loads of iron and other nutrients. It's a brilliant detox food and great for combating candida.

romaine (mild)

The mellow, fresh taste of romaine is not just for salads: 1 to 2 cups (37 to 74g) goes into most blends undetected. Increase your quantity gradually, as overdoing it can lead to a mealy "wet salad" texture and a slight bitterness. Choose compact heads with crisp, unwilted leaves. High in water and low in calories, romaine is intensely hydrating—and great for your skin! It also boosts metabolism, making it an awesome weight-loss food.

radish greens (mild)

With more protein, calcium, and vitamin C than their roots, the leaves of the radish are surprisingly mild in flavor (like lettuce) and go undetected in most blends. My recipes that use them call for 1 cup (37g)—the typical yield of one bunch of radishes. If you're short, substitute spinach. Radish greens are not sold separately, so you'll need to purchase the full bunch. Select radishes with unwilted, bright green leaves, and wash thoroughly to avoid a gritty mouthfeel.

kale (medium)

For mild smoothies, start with 1 cup (25 to 50g) of kale. When adding 2 cups or more, balance the bitterness with sweet fruits like pineapple, mango, berries, grapes, apple, peach, and banana. Tomato, avocado, coconut, chile, and lime or lemon (juice and zest), and bell pepper work well with kale in savory blends. As it's fibrous, kale may not liquefy in a conventional blender. For the smoothest texture, remove the ribs and chop the leaves finely. Or use baby kale, which is softer and less bitter.

chard (medium)

Chard has a mildly bitter, earthy flavor and a salty-lemony note that pairs well with sweet fruits like banana, pineapple, mango, orange, pear, apple, and berries. Used in large quantities, it gets assertive, so start with 1 or 2 leaves. Mint, ginger, and lemon or lime juices will take off the bitter edge, as will sweet fruit juices such as apple, orange, and grape. Chard may turn your blends an unsightly brown hue, so blend it with purple picks—cranberry, pomegranate, or grape juices—or beet, berries, or red grapes for a more lush, vibrant color. Alternatively, embrace the brown—blend in some cacao and go chocolate! Select chard that has firm, dark-green leaves. Chard is extra-perishable as greens go, so store it in the crisper, on top of paper towel or cloth to absorb moisture, and consume within a few days.

collard greens (medium)

Collards have a bitter flavor, so start with 1/2 cup (14g) and mask with sweet fruits like mango, pineapple, peach, berries, banana, apple, and pear. Herbs and spices like mint, citrus, ginger, cinnamon, and cayenne lift and lighten the weight of the collard flavor. However, like chard, collards (even in small amounts) can turn blends an unpalatable brown. If that color isn't appealing, get your dose of collards by blending in milk, cacao, and banana to make a chocolate smoothie. Or pair them with cranberries, pomegranates, grape juice, beet root, berries, or red grapes for pretty, purple pleasure. Regardless of flavor combination, collard greens get even more assertive as a smoothie sits, so enjoy your blend immediately. Select leaves that are a vibrant green, and for the smoothest consistency, remove the thick stem and chop the thick leaves before blending.

beet greens (medium)

Beet greens are spectacular additions to smoothies because they're chock-full of nutrients—more than the roots! Their earthy flavor is easily masked by sweet fruits like pineapple, mango, grapes, and peaches. Start with 1/2 cup (12g) and add to taste. Beet greens added in large amounts can taste like a big old glass of dirt (wash thoroughly to remove the grit), and will turn most blends a dark, muddy brown. Rescue your smoothie from this deathly hue by blending in vibrant crimson characters like cranberry, pomegranate, and grape juices, and beet root, berries, and red grapes. Or go the other direction and hide beet greens in healthy chocolate smoothies that combine milk, cacao, beet root, and banana. Beet greens aren't sold separately, so you'll need to buy whole beets with the greens are attached. Since most people want the leaves chopped off their beets, though, you may find free beet greens at your local farmers' market! The best leaves are dark green and fresh, and are attached to firm, unshriveled roots. The greens wilt very quickly, so store them in the vegetable crisper on paper towel to absorb excess moisture, and consume within 3 days.

bok choy (medium)

Bok choy (also called "pak choi") is not just for stir-fries! You can also use it to create delicious sweet and savory smoothies. With a distinctive flavor, this green gets slightly bitter in large amounts, so blend with sweet fruits like pineapple, mango, banana, apple, pear, citrus, berries, and grapes. Bunches should have dark green leaves on crisp, bright white stalks. This veggie is hardy, and will keep in the crisper or an airtight container for about 5 days.

arugula (strong)

Great as arugula is in salads, it's a brilliant accent in smoothies. But, a little goes a long way. Start small, with 1/8 to 1/4 cup (3 to 6g), and the pleasantly pungent leaves will add a zesty, peppery note. Overdo it and arugula is overpowering and extremely bitter. In balance, it helps temper sweetness, and is magic paired with orange, grapefruit, tangerine, lemon, lime, apple, pear, and berries; it's also wonderful with avocado and cucumber. Choose crisp, young leaves and store at high humidity in the crisper.

dandelion greens (strong)

Don't let the bitterness of this superstar put you off; 1/8 to 1/2 cup (3.5 to 7g) blended with sweet fruits like pineapple, mango, berries, grapes, pear, apple, peach, and banana makes for delicious smoothies. Choose crisp, dark green leaves. Foragers: look for the young greens before the flowers bud—they're less bitter—and always pick in pristine conditions free of pesticides, herbicides, heavy metals, and other toxins or soil pollutants.

Rotate Your Greens

Oxalates and alkaloids, which occur naturally in leafy greens and other plants (and are manufactured by the human body), can be toxic in large amounts. You may have read that oxalates reduce the bioavailability of some nutrients (oxalic acid in spinach, for example, reduces absorption of the iron the green provides); that oxalates cause kidney stones; or that high concentrations of alkaloids have adverse effects including nausea, vomiting, high blood pressure, depression, and anxiety.

Unless you've got a rare health condition like absorptive hypercalciuria type II, enteric hyperoxaluria, or primary hyperoxaluria, indicating strict oxalate and alkaloid restriction, or binge-blend 20 half-pound bags of spinach into one smoothie, you can rest easy: raw leafy greens don't pose a threat to your health.

The majority of kidney stones are calcium oxalate in composition, but research does not show oxalate intake (as opposed to the body's own oxalate manufacture) to be significant in kidney stone development. Recent studies suggest that high intake of protein and calcium and low intake of water are more serious culprits than dietary oxalate in calcium oxalate stone formation. All that said, studies are ongoing, and oxalate remains a controversial topic in clinical nutrition.

Some people steam, blanch, or boil leafy greens to reduce oxalate levels, but I don't cook greens for smoothies. Cooking has minimal effect on their oxalate content, and what little benefit there may be is hardly worth the funky flavor! High heat degrades vitamins and minerals along with fresh taste, and if the greens aren't raw, they don't have their full spectrum of nutrients, including live enzymes.

A measured approach, to avoid excess accumulation of any compounds leafy greens contain, is rotating your greens over the course of the week. Spinach, chard, beet greens, collards, and parsley are the most oxalate-dense, so alternate them with other greens in your smoothies. Drinking ample water, too, and consuming a variety of other nutrient-dense fruits and vegetables, supports assimilation of nutrients and the elimination of toxins.

herbs

Fresh herbs elevate flavors to divine dimensions. Don't try dried—they just don't work in smoothies, and the bitterness is a bummer. Here are my favorites.

basil

I go batty for basil. Depending on the blend, from 2 tablespoons chopped leaves to 1/4 cup (7g) of packed whole leaves adds spectacular flavor to tomato and sweet fruits like watermelon, berries, mango, kiwi, and honeydew.

cilantro

Highly aromatic, with a clean citrus note and a peppery bite, cilantro is fabulous in gazpacho-style smoothies combining tomato, avocado, carrot, sprouts, chile, and salt, or paired with sweet fruits like pineapple, mango, apple, pear, grapes, orange, lime, melon, and papaya.

mint

Mint adds a delightful, fresh aroma and flavor, takes the pungent edge off leafy greens and green powders, balances the earthiness of beets and the cloying effect of sweet fruits, and works true alchemy with ginger. Mint's natural cooling power is great for summer shakes with apple, melon, pineapple, berries, citrus, kiwi, grapes, mango, and peach. Depending on the blend, 1 tablespoon to 1/2 cup (7g) delivers.

parsley

Flat-leaf (aka, Italian) parsley brings a clean, crisp, fresh flavor to fruit blends, especially when paired with pineapple, apple, mango, grapes, and orange. Or use it in savory smoothies featuring tomato, carrot, avocado, and chile. Parsley can be bitter, and in large amounts (some recipes call for 1 bunch), combines best with sweet fruits.

rosemary

A little goes a long way with this one. Generally 3/4 to 1 1/2 teaspoons, finely chopped (for uniform consistency and flavor), strikes a nice balance; much more, and things get bitter. Used sparingly, rosemary adds a mind-blowing accent to blends with a variety of fruits. I love it with watermelon, lemon, orange, tangerine, pineapple, and mango.

spices

If you take one thing from this book, let it be, "Spice it up!" Spices add crazy-amazing flavor and powerful medicinal support. Just do it, and thank me later.

ginger—fresh and ground

Ginger pairs with most fruits and vegetables, adding a citrusy zing and comforting warmth. Fresh ginger provides the best flavor and nutrition, and for uniform results these recipes measure it minced. Depending on the blend, 1/2 to 2 teaspoons strikes a nice balance. Ginger takes the bitter edge off pungent greens, tones down earthy roots, and lifts murky green powders. In some dessert shakes, I use ground dried ginger with sweet spices (but don't substitute it in the recipes that call for fresh). Here, too, easy does it. Start with 1/4 teaspoon and add to taste.

cinnamon

This popular spice pairs well with many flavors. It's delightful blended with chocolate, coconut, banana, berries, apple, pear, orange, mango, peach, carrot, sweet potato, beet, nuts; and with nutmeg, ginger, cardamom, cloves, turmeric, and cayenne pepper. Most blends can handle from 1/8 teaspoon to 1 teaspoon; some can take even more. Intensely warming, cinnamon's a fabulous winter booster.

cardamom

Cardamom adds an exquisite note to smoothies. But its domineering flavor easily overwhelms other ingredients. Start with a pinch; 1/8 teaspoon usually strikes a nice balance. Cardamom is divine paired with rose water, yogurt, milk, and banana, and mind-blowing with peach, apricot, berries, pear, mango, and coconut. It's also spectacular in a chai blend with cinnamon, nutmeg, ginger, and clove. I purchase whole cardamom from Frontier Co-op (see page 241) and grind the seeds as I need them. Pre-ground cardamom lacks full flavor and goes stale quickly.

nutmeg

A little nutmeg goes a long way in a smoothie; too much, and you'll get a bitter, unpalatable taste. With dessert shakes, start with 1/8 to 1/4 teaspoon in combination with other spices like cinnamon, ginger, cardamom, and cloves. Nutmeg pairs well with milks, nuts, chocolate, banana, carrot, and sweet potato. Purchase whole nutmeg and grind or grate as needed for the best flavor.

clove

Clove is a bully spice, so use a light touch. A bare pinch adds a warm aroma and taste to gingerbread, pumpkin pie, carrot cake, and chai smoothies. Clove pairs well with other spices, especially cinnamon, ginger, nutmeg, and cardamom. I love it with cherries, and also in a blend combining cranberry, orange, cinnamon, and fresh ginger. For the best flavor, grind whole cloves as you need them.

cayenne pepper

This ground hot pepper adds kick and healing potential, and as a prebiotic is a great balancing booster for high-sugar blends. Cayenne pairs with almost anything, from apple, grapes, pineapple, mango, citrus, berries, peach, apricot, and pomegranate to bell pepper, tomato, avocado, leafy greens, carrot, and beet. Awesome combined with ginger and cinnamon, it adds a bit of fire to chocolate. It takes the edge off bitter greens and cuts through the earthiness of root vegetables, too.

curry powder

Curry transforms ordinary blends into dimensional dyanamos. The flavor pairs well with fruits like mango, pineapple, peaches, and apricots, especially when blended with coconut milk. Curry mixes vary widely in kick. Start with a pinch and work up to 1/4 to 1/2 teaspoon to hit the sweet—and spicy—spot. To heighten the effect, add a pinch to 1/8 teaspoon of red pepper flakes or cayenne.

red pepper flakes

Like cayenne, red pepper flakes add back-end kick to smoothies, and ease the pungency of leafy greens and beets. Chiles pair well with chocolate and most fruits and vegetables, particularly mango, pineapple, citrus, berries, peach, apricot, pomegranate, grapes, apple, bell pepper, tomato, avocado, and carrot. Start with a pinch; typically 1/8 to 1/4 teaspoon hits the mark.

turmeric

This root is a medicinal master and powerful anti-inflammatory aid. I add it to almost every smoothie for a peppery kick. Because fresh root is not widely available, I've used powdered in these recipes. Start with a pinch; typically 1/8 teaspoon strikes a good balance, but some blends can handle 1/4 teaspoon. I love turmeric paired with citrus, pineapple, strawberries, peach, mango, bell pepper, tomato, carrot, nuts, coconut, and creamy milks. It's also great with ginger and curry powder.

oils

Consuming high-quality oils is essential for health. Fats help protect our organs, nerves, and tissues, and insulate the body from heat and cold. These plant-based oils provide essential fatty acids, deliver fat-soluble vitamins, and fuel us with energy. When adding raw oils to a smoothie, start small, and add to taste.

coconut oil

Cold-pressed virgin coconut oil is a health-promoting rockstar. One teaspoon adds a faint coconut note to blends, and 1 tablespoon becomes assertive. If you're not a fan of coconut, go with a different oil or stick to a scant teaspoon. Increase from there to boost the flavor of other coconut ingredients—water, milk, or meat. Coconut oil works into blends most evenly as a liquid, not solidified.

flaxseed oil

Cold-pressed flaxseed oil is my go-to oil booster. An excellent source of omega-3 essential fatty acids, it's extremely mild in flavor. One tablespoon goes into any blend unnoticed, so this is a fabulous introduction for those wary of oils in shakes.

hemp oil

Cold-pressed hemp oil is an awesome booster with extraordinary health benefits. One teaspoon adds a nutty flavor to any blend. Less is undetectable, and much more brings in a grassy note. Add gradually to taste.

avocado oil

A teaspoon of cold-pressed avocado oil blends into most flavor profiles. Any more and the oil gets assertive, especially in combination with whole avocado, nuts, or nut oils. Savory, gazpacho-style smoothies thrive with 1 tablespoon of avocado oil, but fruit blends don't.

olive oil

A splash of olive oil fortifies and accents flavors in smoothies, even those made with fruit. Most fruit blends tolerate no more than 1 teaspoon; savory blends and spicy fruit profiles can take up to 1 tablespoon. Buy high-quality cold-pressed oil and enjoy it within two months, as phytonutrient and antioxidant levels drop. So use it or lose it!

coconut

Coconut meat, oil, milk, cream, flakes, yogurt, and water (see page 220) have powerful health-promoting qualities and add a touch of magic to smoothies.

coconut yogurt

Yogurt approximates the flavor and texture of ice cream and cream cheese in dessert shakes, is a convenient thickener, and offers probiotics for digestive health and immunity. Go for a natural variety without added sugar-based sweeteners. I like Coyo (see page 241). A quarter-cup (60g) of yogurt adds a tangy accent (heighten with a splash of lemon juice) and 1 cup (240g) delivers a luscious texture and assertive flavor. Yogurt pairs well with most fruits (especially melon, berries, citrus, pineapple, and banana), and with vegetables like carrot, beet, or sweet potato.

creamed coconut

Unsweetened, dehydrated coconut meat ground to a smooth white paste is sold in blocks as creamed coconut. Get Let's Do Organic (see page 241) online, or find other brands at Asian grocers. Creamed coconut goes well in both sweet and savory blends, and you need just 1 tablespoon or a 1-inch (2.5cm) cube for great flavor and creaminess. Cut, grate, or melt a piece and blend it in. The top inch of the block is typically oil, solidified. Add that to smoothies as you would regular coconut oil.

dried coconut

One tablespoon (or more) of unsweetened dried shreds adds accent flavor to smoothies, and enhances the coconut notes in blends using other coconut ingredients. Pick dried coconut that is free of sulfites, preservatives, and enhancers. Soaking dried coconut in the liquid for your shake for at least 15 minutes will soften it for the creamiest texture.

raw coconut meat

The flesh of young Thai coconut adds a rich flavor with a bit of sweetness, and a creamy texture, along with powerful immune boosters. One-half cup to 1 cup (90 to 180g) will do it. Use a Coco Jack (see page 241) to crack open a coconut, drink the water, and scoop out the meat. Or, purchase frozen coconut meat from Exotic Superfoods (see page 241). Coconut pairs especially well with berries, pineapple, mango, citrus, banana, leafy greens, avocado, tomato, carrot, beets, sweet potato, and, of course, chocolate!

superfoods

These nutrient-dense superstars are so powerful you need only a teaspoon or a tablespoon to get your daily dose. I get my superfoods from Navitas Naturals (see page 244). Supercharge your blends with these boosters.

chia

A tablespoon or two of this mildly nutty energizer blends subtly into smoothies. Use as gel (premixed with water), or whole (no grinding needed). Chia delivers protein, fiber, omega-3 fatty acids, calcium, iron, and powerful antioxidant and anti-inflammatory agents. Assisting muscle and tissue building, it's great for workout shakes. Absorbing eight times its weight in water, chia bulks up food in the colon, so it's awesome for cleansing and weight loss. To use chia as a low-fat, sugar-free thickener, chill the blend 15 minutes or more.

flax

A teaspoon of flax meal (brown or golden) goes unnoticed in most blends; a tablespoon adds a mild earthy-nutty flavor. To increase bioavailability and absorption, flaxseeds should be ground. (I use a coffee grinder.) Flaxseeds' soluble fiber thickens a smoothie as it sits, so consume right after blending. A brilliant source of omega fatty acids, fiber, vitamins, minerals, antioxidants, and anti-inflammatory agents, flax boosts immunity and aids digestive regularity. Ladies, hop into the flax! Rich in lignans, it helps balance our hormones.

hemp

For an injection of high-quality protein and other nutrients, I boost smoothies with 1 teaspoon (undetectable in most blends) to 1 tablespoon (which brings on a nutty flavor). Unlike flaxseeds, hemp seeds don't need grinding to increase nutrient bioavailability—just throw them in! Loaded with vitamins, minerals, essential fatty acids, antioxidants, anti-inflammatory agents, fiber, live enzymes, and natural chlorophyll, hemp boosts immunity and promotes heart health. Aiding muscle regeneration and tissue repair, too, it's awesome for workout shakes.

cacao

Get your dessert fix with raw cacao power—the most nutrient-dense form of chocolate. Unsweetened cocoa powder will work in these recipes, but as it's roasted it falls short of the raw stuff in nutrients and antioxidants, and has no live enzymes. Raw cacao is exquisite when blended with creamy milks, coconut, banana, beet, berries, orange, and vegetables like cauliflower, broccoli, and leafy greens. It's an awesome flavor mask for assertive players like collards, chard, and beet greens. A splash of natural extract—vanilla, almond, peppermint, or orange—and a pinch of cayenne or chile powder send a rich chocolate blend into a divine dimension. For most smoothies, 1 tablespoon to ¼ cup (18g) of raw cacao hits the spot. Cacao is a stimulant and can put a strain on the adrenal system, so use it in moderation.

maca

Add mojo and medicinal support to your smoothies with the root known as Peruvian ginseng. Maca, with its strong nutty flavor, likes to be the star, so a little goes a long way. Great costars include banana, cacao, coconut, almond butter, yogurt, and berries. Just 1 teaspoon to 1 tablespoon of maca gives a blend a nice caramel note. Add any more and a lingering bitterness may blast your bliss. Extra banana or some natural sweetener can take that edge off. Maca grows bolder over time, so consume immediately for the most balanced flavor.

Raw maca retains its live enzymes and nutrients. Gelatinized maca is heated, to separate the root's starch. This process destroys live enzymes but activates micronutrients and yields a concentrated powder that is easily digested and assimilated, making this kind of maca a good choice for sensitive stomachs. With a truckload of nutrients and antioxidants, maca boosts immunity, energizes the body, combats stress, and is brilliant for revitalizing the adrenal system. Maca is one of the top plant-based sources of vitamin B12 (great for workout shakes), and helps to metabolize macronutrients, increase endurance, and aid recovery by promoting the regeneration of muscle tissue.

açaí

This low-sugar palm fruit's delicate flavor says tart blackberry with a hint of chocolate. Açaí gives smoothies a delightful creaminess, and pairs beautifully with berries, beet, banana, nut milks, coconut milk, and dates. One tablespoon in a smoothie won't be assertive; 2 tablespoons (or more) and the flavor comes in. Açaí tastes funky with citrus, stone fruits, or melon, and doesn't fare well with most vegetables. Purchase unsweeteend açaí juice, frozen pulp, or freeze-dried powder. I love the pulp, but for convenience, these recipes boost with the powder. Rich in omega fatty acids, protein, fiber, and antioxidants, açaí assists with heart, bone, and digestive health, and is an anti-aging ace.

camu powder

This Amazonian super berry, "nature's vitamin pill," has been documented as the best source of vitamin C. In some parts of South America, you can get fresh camu berries and juice. For the rest of us, the freeze-dried powder (see page 243) is the way forward! One teaspoon has thirty to sixty times as much vitamin C as an orange, more than fifty times as much as a lemon; 1/2 teaspoon provides more than the recommended daily allowance. Since my recipes are designed to make two servings, they call for 1 teaspoon, which doesn't alter flavor; any more starts to tart things up. Camu powder combines beautifully with orange, tangerine, mango, papaya, sweet potato, carrot, peach, apricot, and strawberries. An immunity rock star, it's wonderful for beautiful skin and hair, too.

goji powder

The go-to goji is one of the most nutrient-dense foods on earth. With a tart flavor somewhere between a raisin and a cranberry, goji is available as dried berries, freeze-dried powder, and juice. For convenience and digestibility, I use the powder (see page 243) in smoothies. Dried goji berries are bitter as well as tart, and don't fully pulverize in conventional blenders. A boost of 1 tablespoon is mild enough to go unnoticed. Orange and mango bring out goji's flavor, and the powder is delicious blended with sweet potato, red bell pepper, peach, apricot, and grapefruit. Containing an abundance of nutrients, antioxidants, protein, and healthy fats, this ancient superfood boosts immunity; increases energy; promotes heart, eye, skin, and digestive health; and calms inflammation.

maqui

This dark-purple Patagonian berry contains more antioxidants than any other food. The freeze-dried powder (see page 243) is a versatile booster. It's low in sugar, and its mildly tart, fruity flavor (reminiscent of blackberries and blueberries) pairs well with just about anything—but is easily overwhelmed. Because of its vibrant color, maqui works best blended with purples and reds, like berries and beets, unless you don't mind turning your gorgeous yellow or orange shake a murky brown. Packed with polyphenols and anti-inflammatory agents, maqui is the ultimate anti-aging avenger. Delivering lots of vitamins A, C, and E, just 2 teaspoons has got your immunity covered. This dynamo oxidizes easily, so sip your shakes stat!

pomegranate powder

Unlike pomegranate juice (which is assertive) and pomegranate seeds (only available seasonally and bitter), freeze-dried pomegranate powder (see page 243) is available year-round, delivers the trademark ruby-red color, and has a flavor that harmonizes with virtually any smoothie. A boost of 1 to 2 tablespoons pairs well with orange, tangerine, mango, carrot, sweet potato, peach, apricot, and papaya. With potent antioxidants, phytoestrogens, polyphenols, and fiber, pomegranate powder supports immune function and longevity, and promotes healthy skin and bones and the development of tissues, cells, organs, and rich blood.

spirulina and chlorella

These chlorophyll-rich blue-green algae powders are so pungent that most people gag at just a whiff. Instead of turning your smoothie into a gulp of dirty seawater, cut the murk with mint, lemon, and sweet fruits like banana, pear, apple, mango, and pineapple. Creamy milks, spices, and protein powders mask the blue-greens, too. Start with just a pinch, go to $1/8$ teaspoon, and ease up to $1/2$ teaspoon. The aquarium flavor intensifies in a blend, so drink right up! Purchase "cracked wall" powder, which is the most digestible. These algaes are worth it. Powerful detox agents and chelators, they flush heavy metals from the body and are brilliant for cancer patients, activating the immune system and promoting cell renewal, while easing the effects of radiation and chemotherapy.

wheatgrass

If you who can't stand the taste of wheatgrass juice, or don't have time to make it, add protein-rich freeze-dried powder to a smoothie. Wheatgrass powder adds a clean, crisp note to workout and detox shakes. Start with $1/4$ teaspoon and work up to 1 teaspoon. Most sweet blends with pineapple, mango, grapes, apple, lemon, lime, or honeydew can handle up to 1 teaspoon. Any more and things get grassy. Mint and ginger will tone down the blast of clean-and-green. Then again, some of us like that. Low in calories (and gluten-free), wheatgrass is among the most nutrient-dense foods. With seventy vitamins and minerals, hundreds of live enzymes, chlorophyll, and potent antioxidants, this is a powerful supplement.

flavor enhancers and sweeteners

Here are my go-to "magic" boosters to accent flavors, elevate bland blends, tone down assertive ingredients, and give smoothies an exotic twist.

vanilla

Natural vanilla or its pure extract enhances the flavor of dessert-style smoothies made with chocolate, nuts, and fruit. You can break open a vanilla pod or use vanilla paste. But, to make things economical and accessible, my recipes use liquid vanilla extract. I use the organic, pure, alcohol-free stuff made by Frontier Co-op (see page 241). Imitation vanilla extract and artificial vanilla flavoring are made with sugar and alcohol, and treated with chemicals. If you're using that kind in these recipes, halve the quantity specified and add to taste.

natural extracts

Use liquid extracts of almond, peppermint, orange, lemon, banana, pineapple, and coconut to bring great accent flavors to chocolate smoothies, or to boost the flavor of the corresponding ingredient. Highly potent, a little goes a long way, especially with almond and peppermint extracts. Typically, 1/8 to 1/4 teaspoon is all you need, but some blends can handle more. Add in small increments to taste. Frontier Co-op (see page 241) makes alcohol-free, natural liquid extracts—they're less potent, but healthier.

orange blossom water

Also known as orange flower water, this fragrant liquid is amazing in smoothies. Find it at health food stores, Middle Eastern grocers, and online. I use the Cortas brand (see page 241) to boost the flavor of orange juice, flesh, and zest, and to add a dimensional note to blackberry blends. It's also sensational with creamy milks, nuts, and banana. Start with a tiny splash—1/8 teaspoon—then add to taste, or you may overpower other ingredients.

rose water

Wonderfully fragrant, 1/2 to 1 teaspoon of pure rose water (not rose syrup, which is full of sugar) is exquisite with banana, yogurt, and cardamom, and spectacular with coconut. You can find the Cortas brand (see page 241) at health food stores, Middle Eastern grocers, and online.

stevia

I don't consider this sucrose-free herb a sweetener, which is why recipes containing stevia are classified as unsweetened. Stevia is alkaline and does not alter blood-sugar levels, making it a healthy sugar alternative. Available as crushed leaves, powder, and liquid, stevia is potent—in its pure form, it's about 300 times sweeter than sugar. I use the high-quality, alcohol-free liquid stevia (see page 244) from SweetLeaf and Nu Naturals. (When stevia is produced with alcohol, it's less alkaline, and isn't raw). Both brands offer plain and flavored stevia products that are free of the unpalatable aftertaste I've consistently run into with other brands. Many stevia products contain fillers, so it's a good idea to read labels. Most of my recipes call for plain liquid stevia; one does specify SweetLeaf's English toffee flavor. I typically enhance a smoothie with anywhere from 5 to 20 drops. The "sweet spot" depends on a blend's flavor profile and your preference. A single drop can make the difference, so add stevia drop by drop to taste.

sweeteners

Choose natural sweeteners to fit the personalities of your blends. To keep things consistent (and so you can economically stock your pantry with a set of go-to ingredients), I've created these recipes using pitted dates, maple syrup, and coconut nectar. I use dates a lot because they support base flavors beautifully. Always soak them (see page 6), particularly if you're using a conventional blender, as they can be difficult to incorporate. I love maple syrup for bringing a rich decadence to dessert shakes. Always use pure maple syrup, not maple-flavored swill. You can substitute maple syrup for dates in any of the recipes. As a low-glycemic choice, use coconut nectar in place of maple syrup (but if the shake needs that maple flavor, you'll be missing out). Yacon syrup is another healthy option, but it's a bit pricey and not widely available outside health food stores. For a caramel flavor, lucuma powder is a great raw sweetener. Like yacon, though, lucuma is not widely stocked by retailers. Last but not least are fruit juices like apple, pear, orange, pineapple, and grape (see the juices section on page 220), which add a light sweetness to blends. See the Resources (page 241) for good suppliers of these sweeteners.

resources

COCONUT PRODUCTS

Coconut Secret
coconutsecret.com
Nectar, crystals, ice cream,
aminos.

Coyo
coyo.com
Yogurt, ice cream.

Coco Symbiosis
cocosymbiosis.com
Raw coconut water.

Edward & Sons
edwardandsons.com
Canned coconut milk
and cream; dried,
shredded, and flaked
coconut.

Exotic Superfoods
exoticsuperfoods.com
Raw coconut meat and
water.

Harmless Harvest
harmlessharvest.com
Raw coconut water.

Let's Do Organic
Dried, canned, and creamed
coconut.

Nutiva
nutiva.com
Manna, oil, sugar.

Tropical Traditions
tropicaltraditons.com
Various products.

FLAVOR ENHANCERS AND SWEETENERS

Coconut Secret
coconutsecret.com
Coconut crystals and
coconut nectar.

Maple Valley
maplevalleysyrup.coop
Organic maple syrup and
maple sugar.

Navitas Naturals
navitas.com
Coconut sugar, yacon
syrup, lucuma powder.

Nu Naturals
nunaturals.com
Alcohol-free stevia.

Nutiva
nutiva.com
Organic coconut sugar.

SweetLeaf
sweetleaf.com
Alcohol-free and
flavored stevia.

HERBS, SPICES, FLAVORINGS, AND SEASONINGS

Bragg
bragg.com
Liquid aminos and
apple cider vinegar.

Cortas
amazon.com
Rose water and orange
blossom water.

Edward & Sons
edwardandsons.com
The Wizard's GF
Worcestershire sauce.

Frontier Co-op
frontiercoop.com
Organic dried herbs, spices,
alcohol-free flavors and
extracts.

San-J
san-j.com
Gluten-free tamari.

JUICES AND LIQUIDS

Genesis Today
genesistoday.com
Superfood juices (açai, goji,
noni, mangosteen, sea
buckthorn).

Happy Tree
drinkhappytree.com
Raw Maple Water

Lakewood
lakewoodjuices.com
Variety of organic juices,
including aloe vera juice.

Lily of the Desert
lilyofthedesert.com
Organic aloe vera juice.

Olive Water
olivewater.com
Olive water.

Sibu Beauty
sibubeauty.com
Sea buckthorn juice.

SunnyGem
sunnygemjuice.com
Unsweetened pomegranate
juice.

Trader Joe's
traderjoes.com
Variety of unsweetened
juices.

True Nopal
truenopal.com
Cactus water.

Tsamma Juice
tsammajuice.com
Watermelon juice.

Vertical Water
verticalwater.com
Maple water.

KITCHENWARE
_____

Amco Houseworks
amcohouseworks.com
Juice squeezers.

Coco Jack
coco-jack.com
Coconut cracking tool.

Cutco
cutco.com
Kitchen knives.

Dreamfarm
dreamfarm.com
Kitchen tools, food
storage, spatulas.

Eco Jarz
ecojarz.com
Jars, lids, and stainless
steel straws.

Glass Dharma
glassdharma.com
Glass straws.

Global
global-knife.com
Kitchen knives.

John Boos
johnboos.com
Wooden chopping
boards and blocks.

Kitchen IQ
kitcheniq.com
Citrus zesters, ginger
tool, spice graters.

Klean Kanteen
kleankanteen.com
Stainless steel bottles
and mugs.

Le Creuset
lecreuset.com
Cookware, spatulas, spoons.

Life Factory
lifefactory.com
Glass drink bottles.

Omega Juicers
omegajuicers.com
Juicers.

Oxo
oxo.com
Ice cube trays.

Shun
shun.kaiusaltd.com
Kitchen knives.

Tovolo
tovolo.com
Silicone ice cube molds.

Vitamix Corporation
vitamix.com
Blenders.

Williams-Sonoma
williamssonoma.com
Various kitchen products.

MILKS
_____

Flax USA
flaxusa.com
Flax milk.

Lekithos Inc.
mysunflowerlecithin.com
Sunflower seed lecithin for
homemade milk.

Living Harvest
livingharvest.com
Hemp milk.

One Lucky Duck
oneluckyduck.com
Nut milk bags.

Pacific Natural Foods
pacificfoods.com
Variety of plant-based milks.

Rice Dream
tastethedream.com
Rice milk.

Silk
silk.com
Dairy-free milks (almond,
coconut, cashew, soy).

So Delicious
sodeliciousdairyfree.com
Culinary coconut milk and
other dairy-free milks.

Suncoast Gold
suncoastgold.com.au
Macadamia milk.

NUTS AND SEEDS
_____

Artisana Organics
artisanafoods.com
Organic nut and seed
butters.

Living Tree Community
Foods
livingtreecommunity.com
Nuts, nut butters.

Manitoba Harvest
manitobaharvest.com
Hemp seeds.

Navitas Naturals
Navitasnaturals.com
Raw cashews.

Nutiva
nutiva.com
Hemp, chia seeds.

Nuts.com
nuts.com
Variety of nuts, seeds, nut
butters, and other products.

Ojio
myojio.com
Nuts, sacha inchi seeds,
jungle peanuts.

Raw Nuts and Seeds
rawnutsandseeds.com
Various products.

Sun Butter
sunbutter.com
Nut-free sunflower
seed butter.

Vivapura
vivapura.com
Best nut butters ever.

OILS

Apollo Olive Oil
apollooliveoil.com
Organic extra-virgin olive oil.

Artisana Organics
artisanafoods.com
Coconut oil.

Barleans
barleans.com
Flax oil, borage oil.

Bellavado
bellavado.com
Avocado oil.

Manitoba Harvest
manitobaharvest.com
Hemp oil.

Napa Valley Naturals
napavalleynaturals.com
Organic extra-virgin
olive oil and other oils.

Nutiva
nutiva.com
Organic coconut oil,
hemp oil.

ORGANIC FRESH PRODUCE

Driscoll's
driscolls.com
Organic berries.

Earthbound Farm
ebfarm.com
Leafy greens, fresh fruits
and vegetables.

Kenter Canyon Farms
kentercanyonfarms.com
Organic fresh herbs.

Melissa's Produce
melissas.com
Largest variety of organic
fruits and vegetables.

ORGANIC FROZEN PRODUCE

Earthbound Farm
ebfarm.com
Frozen fruits and
vegetables.

**PROBIOTIC SUPPLEMENTS/
KEFIR SUPPLIES**

Body Ecology
bodyecology.com
Culture starters, cultured
drinks.

Cultures for Health
culturesforhealth.com
Starters, kefir, kombucha,
and fermentation supplies.

GT's Kombucha
synergydrinks.com
Kombucha.

Healing Movement
healingmovement.net
Coconut water kefir.

Kevita
kevita.com
Probiotic drinks.

Solaray
Probiotic supplements.

Tonix Botanical
Solutions
mytonix.com
Coconut water kefir.

VSL#3
shop.vsl3.com
Probiotic supplements.

**PROTEIN AND
GREEN POWDERS**

Garden of Life
gardenoflife.com
Raw powders.

Growing Naturals
growingnaturals.com
Rice and pea powders.

Manitoba Harvest
manitobaharvest.com
Hemp powders.

Nutiva
nutiva.com
Hemp protein.

Sprout Living
sproutliving.com
Raw and sprouted
powders.

Sun Warrior
sunwarrior.com
Protein and ormus
supergreens.

Vega
myvega.com
Great plant-based blends.

SALT

Selina Naturally
celticseasalt.com
Celtic sea salt.

SUPERFOODS

Jing Herbs
jingherbs.com
Herbal tonics and powders.

Miracle Clay
miracleclay.net
Edible clay.

Navitas Naturals
navitasnaturals.com
Superfood powders.

Ojio
myojio.com
Spirulina, chlorella, mesquite, baobab.

Selina Naturally
selinanaturally.com
Organic moringa powder

Vitacost
vitacost.com
World organic liquid
chlorophyll and other
supplements.

TEA

Frontier Co-op
frontiercoop.com
Organic and fair-trade teas.

Guayaki
guayaki.com
Yerba mate.

Harmless Harvest
harmlessharvest.com
Raw cold-brewed namacha.

Numi Tea
numitea.com
Organic teas.

The Republic of Tea
republicoftea.com
Organic teas.

Rishi
rishi-tea.com
Fair-trade teas.

Traditional Medicinals
traditionalmedicinals.com
Herbal and medicinal teas.

Yogi
yogiproducts.com
Herbal and medicinal teas.

WATER

AlkaViva
alkaviva.com
Alkaline water machines.

Castle Rock Water Company
castlerockwatercompany.com
Alkaline glacial water packaged in glass.

Nikken PiMag Waterfall
nikken.com
Water filtration systems.

Phi Sciences
phisciences.com
Crystal Energy "Hunza Water."

pH Miracle Living
phmiracleliving.com/
Puriphy pH water drops.

Santevia
santevia.com
Alkaline jugs and bottles.

acknowledgments

This book and app would not have been possible without the extraordinary Julie Bennett, Henri Clinch, Sharon Bowers, Jess Taylor, and Joe Stallone, who walked every step of this journey with me.

Immeasurable thanks to Emma Campion, Erin Kunkel, Margaux Keres, Kimberly Kissling, Nicole Paizis, Emily Garland, Christine Wolheim, David Bornfriend, Elena Graham, and Maxwell Hibbert for making this smoothie world so beautiful; and to Ranjana Armstrong, Randi Rosenkranz, Aaron Wehner, Hannah Rahill, Michele Crim, Erin Welke, Daniel Wikey, Ali Slagle, Kelly Snowden, Dawn Yanagihara, Jill Greto, Kimberly Snead, Alissa Kleinman, Emily Pollack, Sally Franklin, Milena Schmidt, Katherine McCahill, and Dan Anderson for your dedication to this project.

I'm indebted for the generous support of Vitamix, Earthbound Farm, Navitas Naturals, Exotic Superfoods, Harmless Harvest, Frontier Co-op, Edward & Sons, Let's Do Organic, Selina Naturally, Pacific Foods, the Organic Maple Cooperative, Coconut Secret, SweetLeaf Stevia, NuNaturals, Bella Vado, Barlean's, Vega, Driscoll's, Ruhlin Group, Cutco, Kitchen IQ, and Westin Hotels. A special mention to the heroic Robert Schueller from Melissa's Produce.

I bow to my sensational smoothie-tasting tribe: Richard Parsons, Mikaho Hara, Susan Stitt, Gina Smith, John and Sandra Hanes; Michelle Smith-Aiken and Korey Aiken; Anna Hanson; Debbie and Chuck Pine; Alicia Elliott; Jacque Godwin; Pola, Dave, and Mark Snell; Hillary Huber; Holly, Jason, and Zoey Ojalvo; Jennifer, Scott, Catherine, and Benjamin Ward; Judith Lewis; Karen Kipp and Bobby Herman; Kibby and Scott Miller; Marie-Guy Maynard, and Louis, Tomas, Jacob, and Lucas Subirana; and Elaine and Kathleen Morales.

To Mum, Dad, Kara, Leigh, Alex, Sully, Cookie, and Scott: Your unfailing love and support makes all things possible. To Denise Chamberlain: Consummate kitchen co-conspirator and staunch ally through a zillion blends, I lie at your feet for making me laugh while we faced death by smoothie. And, to my thirsty reader: May these tips and recipes inspire you to slurp your way to sublime smoothie success, and find your perfect blend.

index

Published in the United States by Ten Speed Press,
an imprint of the Crown Publishing Group, a division
of Penguin Random House LLC, New York.
www.crownpublishing.com
www.tenspeed.com

Ten Speed Press and the Ten Speed Press colophon are
registered trademarks of Penguin Random House LLC.

Portions of this work were previously published in
The Blender Girl Smoothies app, published in the United
States by Ten Speed Press, a division of Penguin Random
House LLC, New York, in 2014.

Library of Congress Cataloging-in-Publication Data

Masters, Tess.
The Blender Girl smoothies: 100 gluten-free, vegan
& paleo-friendly recipes / Tess Masters.

    pages cm
Includes bibliographical references and index.
1. Smoothies (Beverages) 2. Vegetable juices.
I. Title. TX817.S636M37 2015
641.8'75—dc23

                                2015003754

Hardcover ISBN: 978-1-60774-8939
eBook ISBN: 978-1-60774-8946

Printed in China

Design by Margaux Keres
Art direction by Emma Campion
Icon design by Maxwell Hibbert

10 9 8 7 6 5 4 3 2 1

First Edition